ARE YOU TIRED OF TELEVISION?
BORED BY THE MOVIES?
CONFUSED BY THE DAILY PAPERS?

If you are, we don't blame you. We feel the same way ourselves. What's more, we didn't take it lying down. We stood up, hour after hour, day after day, putting together this great collection.

NO MORE FUZZY TUNING!
NO MORE POPCORN ON YOUR SEAT!
NO MORE EYESTRAIN!

Here's all the entertainment and information you need . . . and YOU can take it lying down . . . with

THE
BEDSIDE
MAD

HOMOGENIZED SALAMI

WILLIAM M. GAINES'S

THE
BEDSIDE
MAD ™

ibooks
new york
www.ibooksinc.com

DISTRIBUTED BY SIMON & SCHUSTER, INC

Front cover painting by Kelly Freas

Special thanks to:
Grant Geissman;
Nick Meglin (*MAD* Magazine)

An ibooks, inc. Book

Distributed by Simon & Schuster, Inc.
1230 Avenue of the Americas, New York, NY 10020

ibooks, inc.
24 West 25th Street
New York, NY 10010

The ibooks World Wide Web Site Address is:
http://www.ibooksinc.com

Visit www.madmag.com

ISBN 0-7434-5910-5
First ibooks, inc. printing June 2003
10 9 8 7 6 5 4 3 2 1

Printed in the U.S.A.

CONTENTS

Introduction by Grant Geissman . . . vii

Horror Department
    Outer Sanctum! . . . 6

Juvenile Western Department
    The Lone Stranger Rides Again! . . . 30

Scenes We'd Like to See Department—I . . . 51

Navy Department
    The Cane Mutiny! . . . 58

TV Department
    Medical . . . 76

Report from Abroad—I . . . 95

Adult Western Department
    'Hah! Noon!' . . . 96

Scenes We'd Like to See Department—II . . . 117

Report from America Department
    Restaurant! . . . 122

Poetry Department
    Casey at the Bat! . . . 140

Literary Classics Department
    Robinson Crusoe . . . 158

Report from Abroad—II . . . 179

Science Department
    Slow Motion! . . . 180

Report from Abroad—III . . . 192

INTRODUCTION
by Grant Geissman

Just when you thought it was safe to go back into the bookstore, here comes *The Bedside MAD*, the sixth book in the series of anniversary reprints—published by ibooks—of the early *MAD* paperbacks.

The original version of *The Bedside MAD* appeared in April 1959, and was the first *MAD* paperback to be issued under the Signet Books imprint. Although it was actually the brainchild of Ballantine Books to offer *MAD* paperbacks in the first place, after five books *MAD* publisher Bill Gaines elected to move the line to Signet Books (later called New American Library), who offered much higher advances and a larger print run than did Ballantine.

The title *The Bedside MAD* was a spin on the various "bedside reader" paperback compilations that were then in vogue. On the cover of *The Bedside MAD* is a first for a *MAD* paperback: an original painting commissioned especially for the book, rendered by beloved illustrator Kelly Freas, who was the magazine's regular cover artist at the time. (Covers to the earlier *MAD* paperbacks were essentially created out of material that had previously appeared in *MAD*.)

Although by 1959 *MAD* had long graduated to its now-familiar magazine format (selling for "25¢— Cheap!"), with but two exceptions the material appearing here was taken from *MAD*'s original incarnation as a 10¢ comic book (created, written, and laid out for the artists by the triple threat artist/writer/editor Harvey Kurtzman).

Opening the book is "Outer Sanctum!" (*MAD* #5, June–July 1953, illustrated by Bill Elder), Kurtzman's parody of both the long-running radio thriller *Inner Sanctum* and of the stories in E.C.'s horror comics. The story is an all-time Bill Elder classic. Here Elder manages to combine the look and feel of an E.C. horror tale with his own antic, signs-on-the-wall style. *Outer Sanctum* actually got *MAD* publisher Bill Gaines in a lot of hot water with some of his wholesalers. Elder had inserted a sign in the second panel (found here on page eight) that read "Nice, clean, fat errand boy wanted—J. Ghoul." As Gaines recalled to comics historian John Benson: "You and I know what the nice, fat errand boy was wanted for; he was wanted to be eaten. But not the wholesalers! They *knew* he was wanted for *sexual perversion*. They really believed it. What do wholesalers know about ghouls?"

"The Lone Stranger Rides Again!" (*MAD* #8, December 1953-January 1954, illustrated by Jack Davis) is Kurtzman's second take on *The Lone Ranger*, the popular and long-running radio and television series. His first satire of *The Lone Ranger* appeared in *MAD* #3 (February-March 1953), and can be found in the first volume in this series, *The MAD Reader*. The story's ending, incidentally, is a typically Kurtzman-esque twist.

"Scenes We'd . . . Like to See!" is a much-truncated version of a feature that originally appeared in *MAD* #23 (May 1955, illustrated by Jack Davis). The original version presented not only the "surrounded fort scene" that appears here, but also a "kissing scene," a "fencing scene," an "escape from the Nazis scene," and a "bump him off scene." Obviously the original, uncut version plays better. The second "Scenes We'd Like to See" appearing here (titled "The Musketeer Who Failed to Get the Girl") is actually a stylistic cousin to the first, and is from *MAD* #27 (April 1956), its fourth issue as a 25¢ magazine. This feature was not written by Kurtzman, but was both written and illustrated by Phil Interlandi. Interlandi did about nine of these "Scenes We'd Like to See" pages for the early magazine version of *MAD*, and then went on to a long career as a cartoonist for *Playboy*.

"The Cane Mutiny!" (*MAD* #19, January 1955, illustrated by Wallace Wood) is Kurtzman's spin on the *The Caine Mutiny*, the 1954 movie version of Herman Wouk's Pulitzer Prize-winning novel. The film starred such heavyweight actors as Humphrey Bogart (as Captain Queeg, parodied here as "Captain Kweeg"), Fred MacMurray, Van Johnson, E.G. Marshall, and Lee Marvin. Unfortunately, Wallace Wood's art is uncharacteristically stiff and, for the most part, his caricaturing of the actors is, disappointingly, only passable.

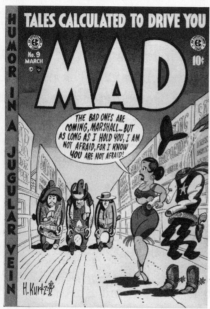

TALES CALCULATED TO DRIVE YOU
MAD
HUMOR IN A JUGULAR VEIN
No. 9
MARCH
10¢
THE BAD ONES ARE COMING, MARSHALL... BUT AS LONG AS I HOLD YOU, I AM NOT AFRAID, FOR I KNOW YOU ARE NOT AFRAID!
H. Kurtz
Kurtzman's "Hah! Noon!' cover to MAD *#9 (February-March 1954).*

A movie parody that fares far better is "Hah! Noon!" (*MAD* #9, February-March 1954, illustrated by Jack Davis), Kurtzman's lampoon of the classic 1952 motion picture *High Noon*, starring Gary Cooper and Grace Kelly. Cooper won an Oscar for his portrayal of a town sheriff who, on his wedding day, has to face an outlaw band that has sworn to take vengeance against him—at high noon, naturally. Oscars also went to composer Dimitri Tiompkin and lyricist Ned Washington for the song "Do Not Forsake Me, Oh My Darlin'," which threads itself through both the movie and through Kurtzman's parody. Davis, always a master with cowboys and western settings, was the perfect choice to tackle this story, and here he achieves a "cartoony" but on-target rendering of Gary Cooper.

"Medical" is from *MAD* #28 (July 1956, illustrated by Bill Elder), the fifth issue of *MAD* as a 25¢ magazine, and the last to be edited by Harvey Kurtzman before he jumped ship—although some Kurtzman-edited pieces appeared for several issues beyond that. (See the introduction to the ibooks edition of *Utterly MAD* for an in-depth look at Kurtzman's departure from the magazine and the reasons behind it). "Medical" spoofs *Medic*, which ran on NBC from September 1954 to November 1956. *Medic* was an early television forerunner to such latter-day doctor shows as *St. Elsewhere* and *ER*. The show starred then-newcomer Richard Boone as Dr. Konrad Styner, and was a

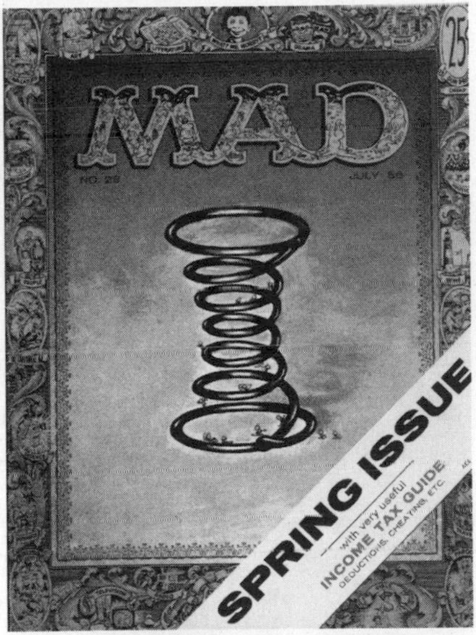
MAD
SPRING ISSUE
with very useful
INCOME TAX GUIDE
DEDUCTIONS, CHEATING, ETC.

The cover of the famously late "Spring issue" of MAD *(#28), that actually didn't appear until the summer of 1956. This was the final issue of* MAD *to be edited by the perennially deadline-challenged Kurtzman.*

trailblazer in TV realism, shot in real hospitals and graphically depicting operations, often employing real doctors and nurses.

The three "Report from Abroad" pieces in this book originally appeared in *MAD* #15 (September 1954), *MAD* #16 (October 1954), and *MAD* #19 (January 1955) as one-page fillers. As Kurtzman has often said of such experiments, "We were desperate to fill pages."

THE BEDSIDE
#6
MAD
75¢ 74-042 WARNER PAPERBACK LIBRARY

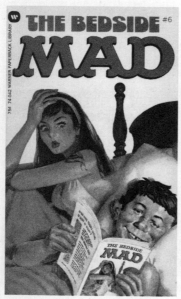

Norman Mingo's cover for the May, 1973 reissue.

"Restaurant!" (*MAD* #16, October 1954) is a Bill Elder tour-de-force, with its chaotic splash panel, surly waiters, the charming Sturdley family, and the bratty-yet-adorable kid in the next booth. And Kurtzman is at the top of his game here, presenting a slice of New York City lifestyle that would otherwise have been unimaginable to readers in the midwest say, or in California. Incidentally, the caption above the title of this piece was changed for its paperback appearance. It originally read: "Following the usual *MAD* [read

"Kurtzman"] policy of experimenting with new things and thereby coming closer to ruin, we introduce a new feature, dealing with various phases of life in America." In light of Kurtzman's subsequent departure from the magazine and his many terminally uncommercial (but artistically successful) endeavors that followed, the "closer to ruin" line in the caption is remarkably self-revelatory.

"Casey at the Bat!" (*MAD* #6, August-September 1953) is Jack Davis's take on the enduring Ernest Lawrence Thayer poem of the same name. This was actually the first time Kurtzman presented a well-known poem in *MAD*, but it wouldn't be the last; several other classics would later be given the *MAD* treatment, including Edgar Allan Poe's "The Raven," H. Antoine D'Arcy's "The Face Upon the Floor," and H. W. Longfellow's "Paul Revere's Ride." For "Casey at the Bat!," it would appear that Kurtzman simply transferred Thayer's original verse to the art boards, and instructed Davis to have his way with it—albeit with the standard Kurtzman proviso to follow his tissue-paper layouts for pacing.

Kurtzman skewers another literary classic in "Robinson Crusoe!" (*MAD* #13, July 1954, illustrated by Bill Elder). Elder's background signs are again in plentiful supply. Note also his use of a clipped-out photo of Burt Lancaster and Deborah Kerr from the famous "beach love scene" in *From Here to Eternity* (found here in the second panel of page 163), which echoes again in the second panel of page 169 with a drawing of two skeletons in a lover's embrace.

"Slow Motion!" originally appeared in *MAD* #21 (March 1955, illustrated by Jack Davis). Appearing here is most of the original story; the rest of it (a look at a ski jumper) can be found in *Inside MAD*, the third book in this series. "Slow Motion" is one of Kurtzman's trademark "side-by-side" comparisons, this one involving what the naked eye sees and what the slow motion camera reveals.

And if you're not quite done rotting your brain after finishing this book, fear not: up next from ibooks is a facsimile edition of *Son of MAD*, originally published in October 1959. Even *more* classic *MAD*ness is coming your way! Potrzebie!

Grant Geissman *is the author of* Collectibly MAD, *(Kitchen Sink Press, 1995), and co-author with Fred von Bernewitz of* Tales of Terror! The EC Companion *(Gemstone/Fantagraphics, 2000). He compiled and annotated the "best of" volumes* MAD About the Fifties *(Little, Brown, 1997),* MAD About the Sixties *(Little, Brown, 1995),* MAD About the Seventies *(Little, Brown, 1996), and* MAD About the Eighties *(Rutledge Hill Press, 1999). He also compiled and wrote liner notes for* MAD Grooves *(Rhino, 1996), contributed the introduction to* Spy vs. Spy: The Complete Casebook *(Watson-Guptill, 2001), and wrote the introductions to the 50th anniversary editions of* The MAD Reader, MAD Strikes Back!, Inside MAD, Utterly MAD, *and* The Brothers MAD *(ibooks, 2002). When not reading* MAD, *Geissman is a busy Hollywood studio guitarist, composer, and "contemporary jazz" recording artist, with 11 highly regarded albums released under his own name.*

HORROR DEPT.: FOR HEAVEN'S SAKE! DROP THIS BOOK! GET RID OF IT! BURY IT! DO ANYTHING ONLY DON'T LISTEN TO THIS STORY! FOR IN FRONT OF YOU IS A DOOR, BEHIND WHICH LIES A STORY THAT WILL DO THINGS . . . STRANGE THINGS . . . TO YOU . . . TO YOUR MIND! . . . FOR THIS IS THE INNER DOOR TO THE . . .

OUTER SANCTUM!

6

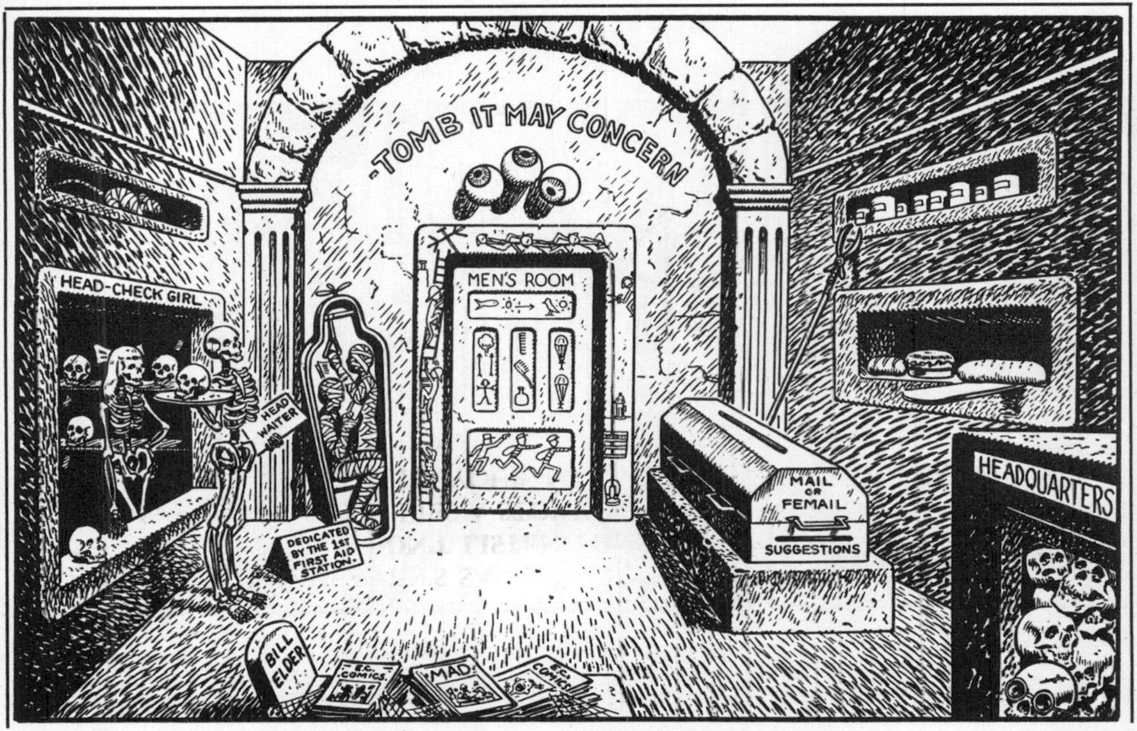
-TOMB IT MAY CONCERN
HEAD-CHECK GIRL
HEAD WAITER
MEN'S ROOM
DEDICATED BY THE 1ST FIRST AID STATION.
MAIL OR FEMAIL
SUGGESTIONS
HEADQUARTERS
BILL ELDER
E.C. COMICS.
MAD
E.C. COMICS

NO TIPPING!
-ADVERTISEMENT -NICE, CLEAN, FAT ERRAND BOY WANTED J. GHOUL
C. O. D.
R. I. P.
L. S. M. F. T.
CHECKS CASHED
SQUEEEEEEEEEEEEEEEEEEEEEEEEEE
GO SLOW - GHOUL ZONE.
TRY ADLERS COCKTAILS -AT LAST YOU CAN GET HIGHER THAN SHE CAN.
MENU
HANDS PRESSED WHILE U WAIT.
CONT-IN-UED.

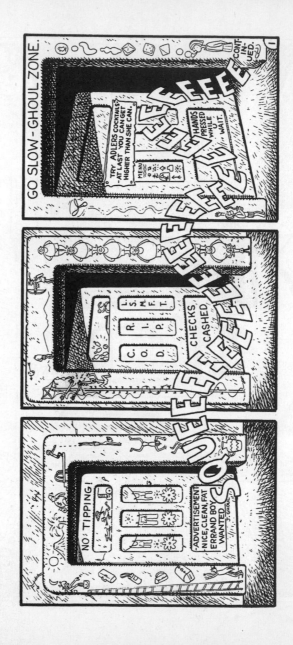

CONT-IN-UED.
WANTED
A NICE FAT OLD LADY WITH HIGH BLOOD PRESSURE.
I.M.A. VAMPIRE
BUTTER MILK
OIL
CHICKEN FAT
BACON GREASE
GOOD EVENING! THIS IS RAMON, YOUR GHOST... I MEAN... HOST! COME IN, I'VE BEEN WAITING FOR YOU!
SQUEEK! SQUEEK

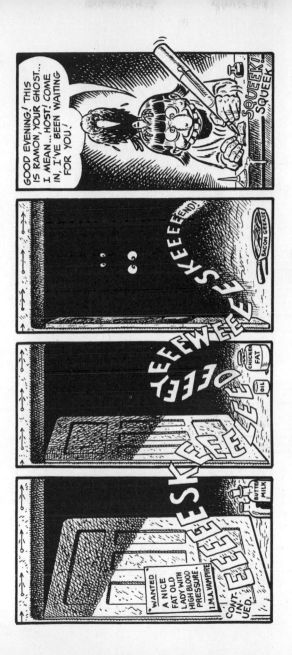

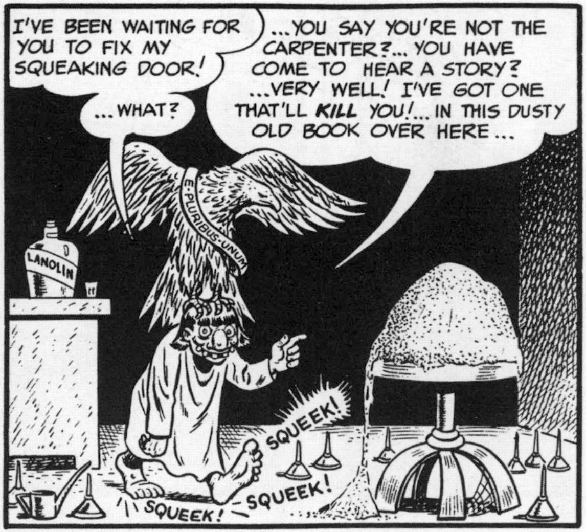
I'VE BEEN WAITING FOR YOU TO FIX MY SQUEAKING DOOR!
...WHAT?
...YOU SAY YOU'RE NOT THE CARPENTER?... YOU HAVE COME TO HEAR A STORY? ...VERY WELL! I'VE GOT ONE THAT'LL KILL YOU!... IN THIS DUSTY OLD BOOK OVER HERE...
LANOLIN
E-PLURIBUS-UNUM
SQUEEK!
SQUEEK!
SQUEEK!
SQUEEK!

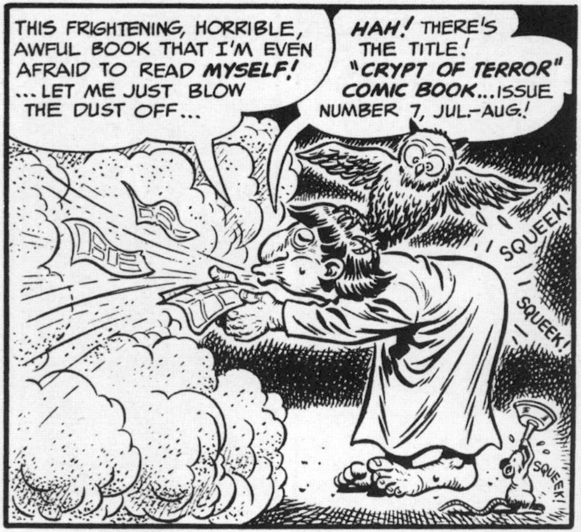
THIS FRIGHTENING, HORRIBLE, AWFUL BOOK THAT I'M EVEN AFRAID TO READ MYSELF! ...LET ME JUST BLOW THE DUST OFF...
HAH! THERE'S THE TITLE! "CRYPT OF TERROR" COMIC BOOK...ISSUE NUMBER 7, JUL.-AUG.!
SQUEEK!
SQUEEK!
SQUEEK!

A RARE OLD COMIC BOOK FROM MY LIBRARY OF **E.C.** COMIC BOOKS SOLD ON NEWSSTANDS EVERYWHERE! YAY!
NOW STICK AROUND, KID, WHILE I PROCEED TO DESTROY YOUR MIND!
CASTOR OIL
SQUEEK!
SQUEEKEEEE

HAH! HERE WE ARE! THIS STORY IS ABOUT A ***THING!*** A HORRIBLE SHAPELESS ***THING!*** NOT VEGETABLE, MINERAL OR ANIMAL... JUST A ***THING!***
THIS STORY WILL GIVE YOU SOME***THING*** TO ***THING*** ABOUT!
...GET IT? ***THING... THINK?*** ...AHEM!
LET'S SEE NOW! OUR STORY BEGINS...
SQUEEK
SQUEEK
COD LIVER OIL
OLIVE OIL
2

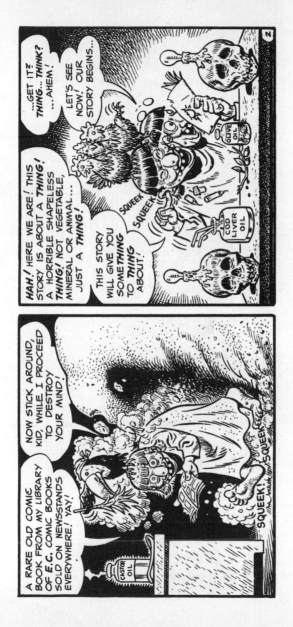

12

...JUST BEYOND THE LOUISIANA BAYOUS IN THE DEPTHS OF MYSTERIOUS, UNEXPLORED, UNPENETRABLE, STEAMING, SWEATY, DISGUSTING OKEEFENOKEE SWAMP!

OKEEFENOKEEFENOKEE SWAMP, WHERE THE WORLD STOOD STILL! NOT A SIGN OF LIFE...*LOOK, PIC* OR *QUICK!* ONLY A TUMBLE DOWN SHACK PROPPED UP WITH A SINGLE BROOMSTICK!

INSIDE THE SHACK, ALSO PROPPED UP BY A BROOMSTICK, WORKED THE 'PROFESSOR'!

YES...A MAN WITH A BRILLIANT MIND WORKED, ALONE IN THE SWAMP!

...WORKED FRANTICALLY AMIDST HIS BUBBLING RETORTS AND TEST TUBES!

WORKED AGAINST TIME....NOW *THE WHOLE WORK WAS DONE! THE MIXTURE WAS READY!*

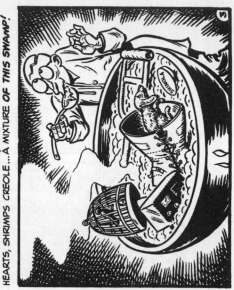

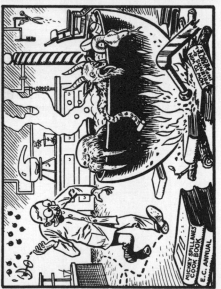

DOWNING THE DRY MARTINI COCKTAIL AT ONE GULP, THE 'PROFESSOR' TURNED TO THE HUGE VAT THAT HELD THE CONTENTS OF A LIFETIME OF RESEARCH, BOILING AND BUBBLING...
MICKEY SPILLANES' COOK BOOK
E.C. ANNUAL
HOW TO WIN FRIENDS & INFLUENTIAL PEOPLE.
...A RECIPE HE'D BEEN GIVEN BY THE OLD CAJUN WITCH WOMAN! CROCODILES' WARTS, CHOPPED UP ZOMBIE HEARTS, SHRIMPS CREOLE...A MIXTURE OF THIS SWAMP!
SHINOLA
3

AND THIS WAS WHY THE 'PROFESSOR' HAD HIDDEN HIMSELF FROM THE *SCOFFING* WORLD! "***SKOFF, SKOFF!***" THEY HAD SKOFFED! '***NO MAN CAN CREATE LIFE!***'

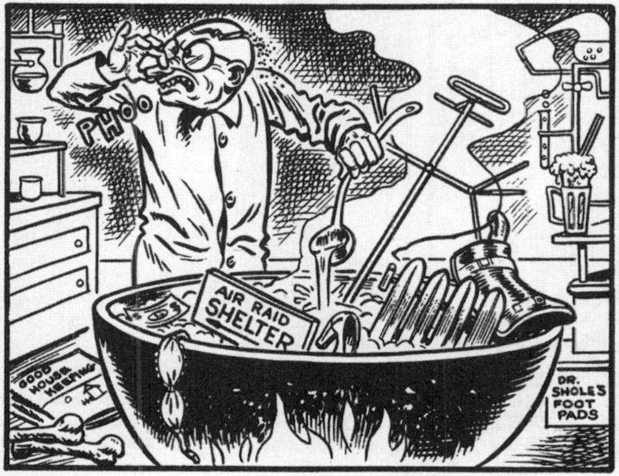
PHOO
AIR RAID SHELTER
GOOD HOUSE KEEPING
DR. SHOLE'S FOOT PADS

SUDDENLY THE SCENT OF MANY *MASHED* POLECATS DRIFTED FROM THE *MIXTURE!*... IN A FLASH, A LIFETIME OF RE-SEARCH WAS SPILLING OUT THE WINDOW!

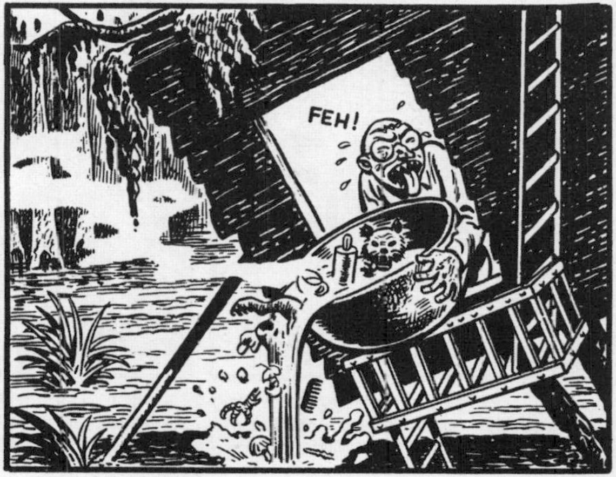
FEH!

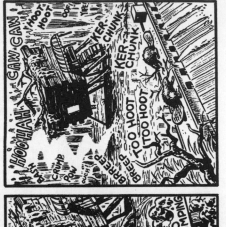

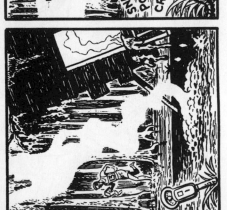

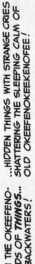

...SPILLED OUT THE WINDOW WHERE IT LAY...COMBINING WITH THE SWAMP WATERS IN A FESTERING MISH-MOSH!
NIGHT FELL!... NIGHT ON THE OKEEFENOKEEKEE SWAMP! SOUNDS OF THINGS... MOVING THROUGH THE BACKWATERS!
K-I-I
KEE
KOO
KOO
SNAP!
POP!
CRACKLE!
NO DUMPING
...HIDDEN THINGS WITH STRANGE CRIES SHATTERING THE SLEEPING CALM OF OLD OKEEFENOKEEKENOFEE!
HOOHAH
CAW CAW
HOOT-HOOT
BASH
CRUMP
POW
OUCH!
OOF!
YIPE!
KER-CHUNK
BRREEP
BREEP
TOO HOOT
TOO HOOT
KER-CHUNK

GREW! STOOD UP! ERECT! A HORRIBLE STANDING GLOB OF SWAMP THING! THERE WAS NOTHING TO CALL IT BUT... HEAP!

...AND... BENEATH THE PROFESSOR'S WINDOW... THE MIXTURE CONTINUED TO PULSATE AND QUIVER WHERE IT HAD LAIN... PULSATED... QUIVERED... AND GREW!

18

...FOR THE 'PROFESSOR' WAS TRULY THIS 'HEAP'S' FATHER! AND AS 'HEAP' EMBRACED HIM IN ITS SLIMEY BANANA PEEL AND TIN CAN ENCRUSTED ARMS, THE EVIL PROFESSOR GOT A HORRID IDEA!

WHEN THE 'PROFESSOR' WOKE UP HE FOUND *IT!*...'HEAP', STANDING OUTSIDE THE DOOR. AND FROM SOMEWHERE INSIDE THIS 'HEAP' CAME A CROAK...THAT SOUNDED LIKE...'PAPA'!

NO PEDDLERS

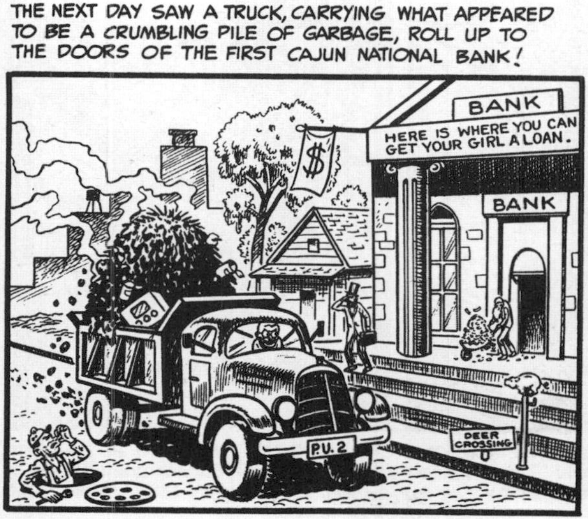
THE NEXT DAY SAW A TRUCK, CARRYING WHAT APPEARED TO BE A CRUMBLING PILE OF GARBAGE, ROLL UP TO THE DOORS OF THE FIRST CAJUN NATIONAL BANK!
BANK
HERE IS WHERE YOU CAN GET YOUR GIRL A LOAN.
$
BANK
DEER CROSSING
P.U. 2

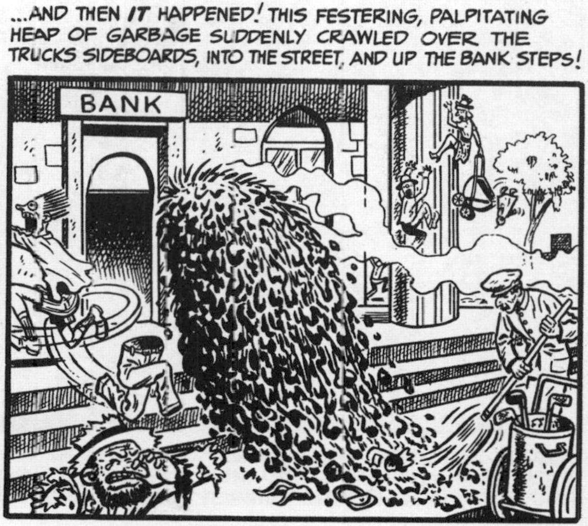
...AND THEN *IT* HAPPENED! THIS FESTERING, PALPITATING HEAP OF GARBAGE SUDDENLY CRAWLED OVER THE TRUCKS SIDEBOARDS, INTO THE STREET, AND UP THE BANK STEPS!
BANK

THEN...LIKE A HUGE AMOEBA, THIS 'HEAP' SLATHERED INTO THE TELLER'S CAGE AND SCOOPED UP THE CASH!... PHEW!
SNIFF
FAROUK ENTERPRIZES
ITS WORK WAS DONE! ***IT*** POURED OUT THE ENTRANCE, UNMINDFUL OF THE HAIL OF BULLETS FROM THE GUARDS!
POW
ARRID
BAM
POW
MUM
CLORETS
BANG
LEAVING A TRAIL OF ORANGE PEELS AND DEAD CATS, IT GOT BACK IN THE TRUCK AND WAS GONE! ***HEAP HAD STRUCK!***
5

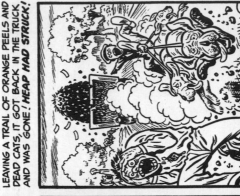

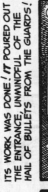

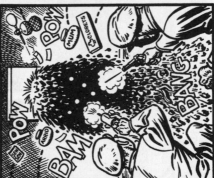

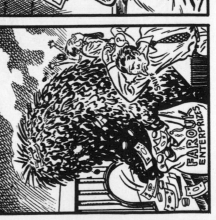

BACK IN THE STEAMING MESSY OL' OKEEFENOKEEDOKEE SWAMP, THE 'PROFESSOR' WAS SOON ROLLING IN DOUGH! HIS 'HEAP' WAS FOLLOWING INSTRUCTIONS WELL!

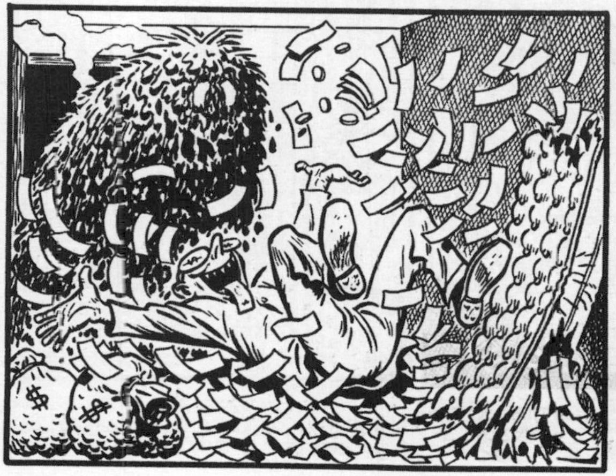

IT WAS EASY TO KEEP 'HEAP' HAPPY! AN OLD DECAYED FISH ...COLD, WET COFFEE GROUNDS...A BIT OF DRIPPING NEWS-PAPER THAT WAS USED TO LINE THE GARBAGE PAIL...

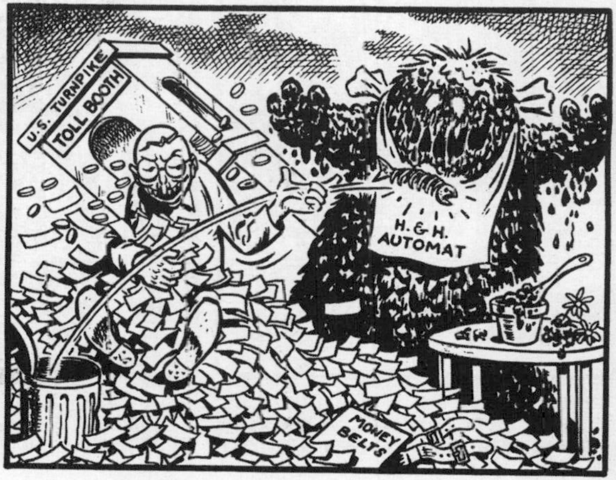
U.S. TURNPIKE
TOLL BOOTH
H. & H. AUTOMAT
MONEY BELTS

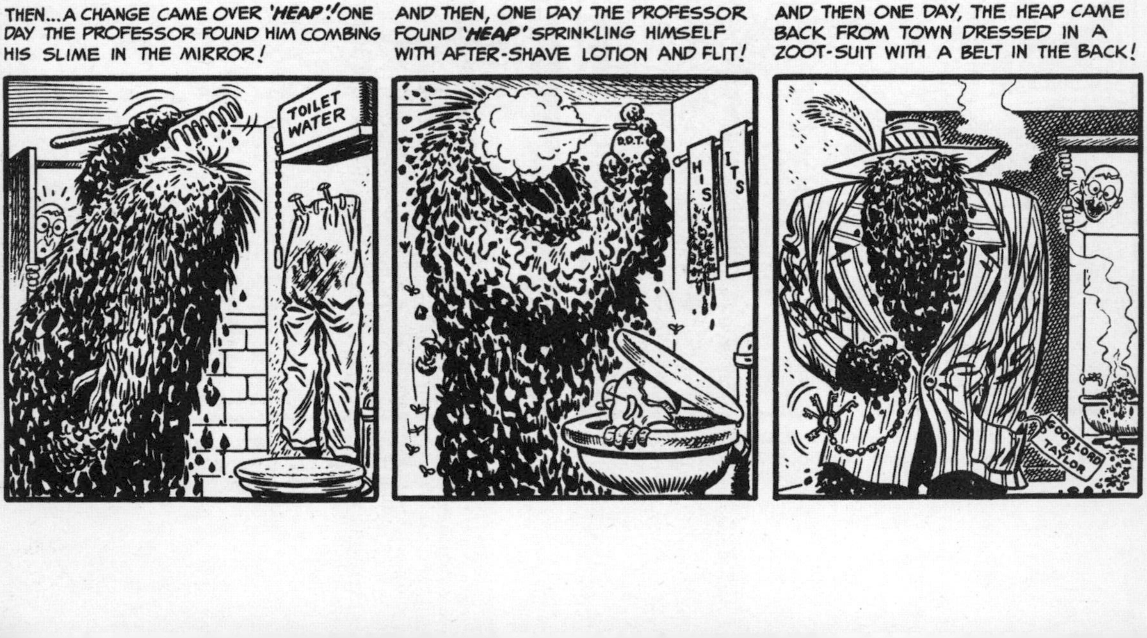
THEN...A CHANGE CAME OVER 'HEAP'! ONE DAY THE PROFESSOR FOUND HIM COMBING HIS SLIME IN THE MIRROR!
TOILET WATER
AND THEN, ONE DAY THE PROFESSOR FOUND 'HEAP' SPRINKLING HIMSELF WITH AFTER-SHAVE LOTION AND FLIT!
D.D.T.
HIS
ITS
AND THEN ONE DAY, THE HEAP CAME BACK FROM TOWN DRESSED IN A ZOOT-SUIT WITH A BELT IN THE BACK!
GOOD LORD & TAYLOR

IN BACK OF THE PROFESSOR'S SHACK LAY A PIECE OF THE PROFESSOR'S GARBAGE, ACCUMULATED THROUGH THE YEARS! BY GEORGE...THIS WAS A *FEMALE GARBAGE HEAP!*

ALL THIS COULD ONLY·HAVE ONE AWFUL·MONSTROUS, HORRI-BLE CONCLUSION....'HEAP' WAS IN *LOVE!* THAT EVENING, THE 'PROFESSOR' FOLLOWED 'HEAP' WHO LOOKED HEP!

—TO AVOID
THAT RUNDOWN
FEELING—
STAY ON THE
CURB!

BUS STOP

THE PROFESSOR KNEW WHAT HAD TO BE DONE! WHEN *'HEAP'* CAME TO LOOK AT HIS BELOVED GARBAGE PILE THE NEXT EVENING... IT WAS BURNED TO THE GROUND!

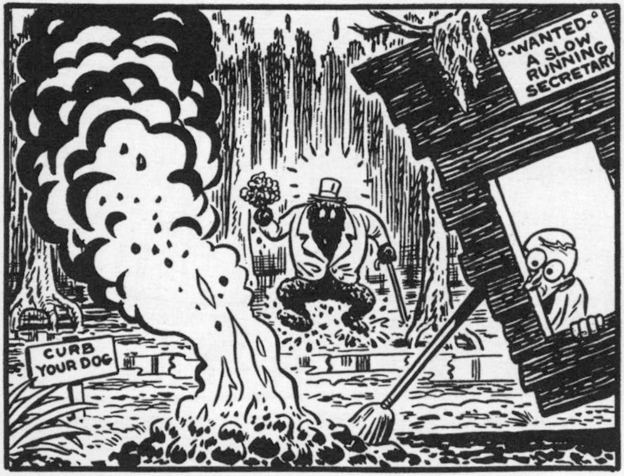
WANTED- A SLOW RUNNING SECRETARY
CURB YOUR DOG

AN ODD CRY LIKE A STEPPED-ON CAT CAME FROM THE TIN CANNED DEPTHS OF *'HEAP,'* AND IN A MAD LOVER'S FRENZY KICKED AWAY THE SINGLE BROOMSTICK...

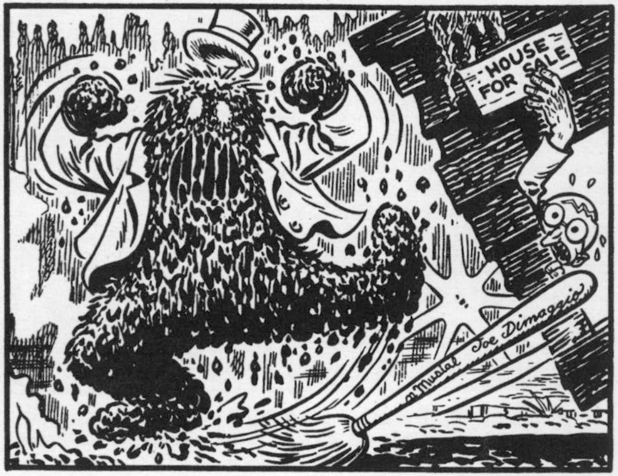
HOUSE FOR SALE
Joe Dimaggio

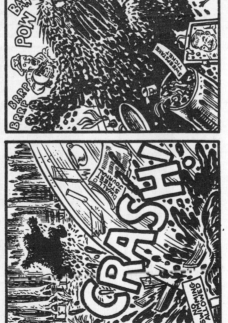

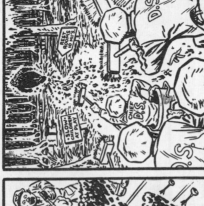

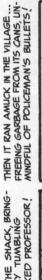

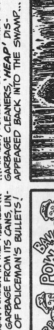

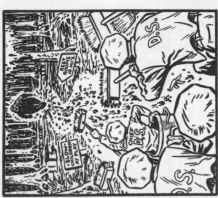

...THAT SUPPORTED THE SHACK, BRINGING THE LABORATORY TUMBLING DOWN ON THE WICKED PROFESSOR!
CRASH!
WALL STREET JOURNAL
NO SWIMMING ALLOWED
THEN IT RAN AMUCK IN THE VILLAGE... FREEING GARBAGE FROM ITS CANS, UNMINDFUL OF POLICEMAN'S BULLETS!
BRRRP BRRRP
POW
BANG
SWEEPSTAKE TICKET
...FINALLY, PURSUED BY A DRAGNET OF GARBAGE CLEANERS, 'HEAP' DISAPPEARED BACK INTO THE SWAMP...
SLOW CHILDREN AT PLAY
REST ROOMS 10 MI'S.
CHIEF D.S.
D.S.
D.S.

...NEVER TO BE SEEN AGAIN!...SOME SAY WHEN THE MOON IS FULL YOU CAN SEE ***IT*** WANDERING OVER THE CITY DUMP, SEARCHING FOR A CERTAIN LITTLE GARBAGE PILE!

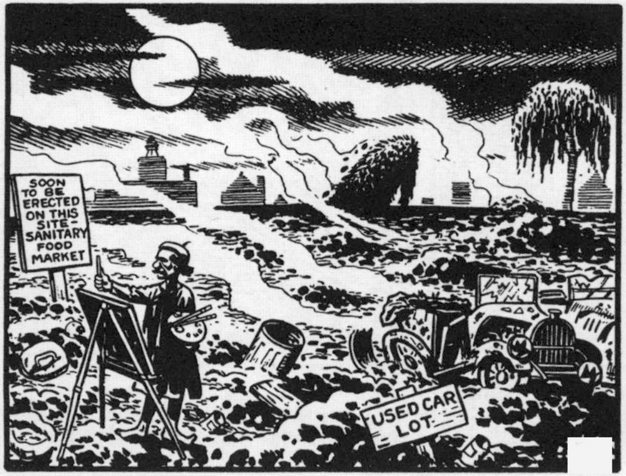
SOON TO BE ERECTED ON THIS SITE- SANITARY FOOD MARKET
USED CAR LOT

SOME SAY ***IT FOUND*** THAT CERTAIN LITTLE GARBAGE PILE... AND WHEN THE MOON IS FULL, YOU CAN SEE THEM BEING FOLLOWED BY ***TINY*** LITTLE GARBAGE PILES!

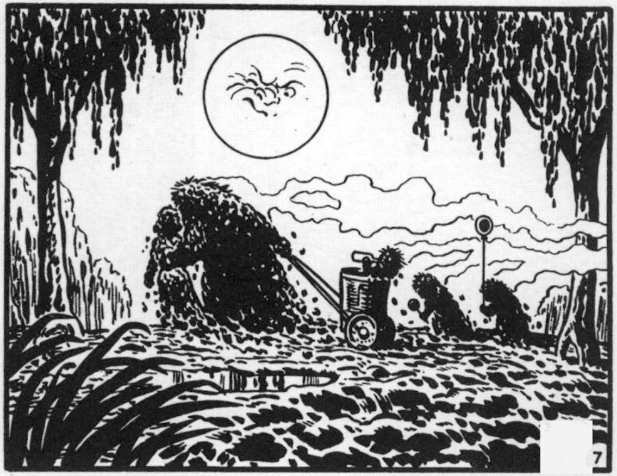

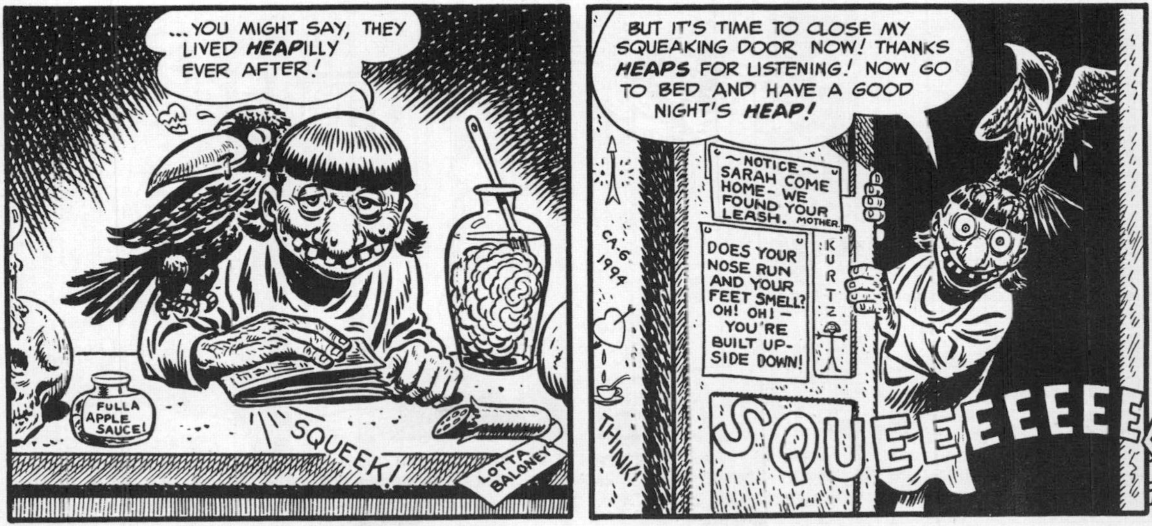
...YOU MIGHT SAY, THEY LIVED HEAPILLY EVER AFTER!
FULLA APPLE SAUCE!
SQUEEK!
LOTTA BALONEY
BUT IT'S TIME TO CLOSE MY SQUEAKING DOOR NOW! THANKS HEAPS FOR LISTENING! NOW GO TO BED AND HAVE A GOOD NIGHT'S HEAP!
~NOTICE~ SARAH COME HOME- WE FOUND YOUR LEASH. MOTHER.
DOES YOUR NOSE RUN AND YOUR FEET SMELL? OH! OH! - YOU'RE BUILT UP-SIDE DOWN!
KURTZ
CA-6 1994
THINK!
SQUEEEEEEEEEEE

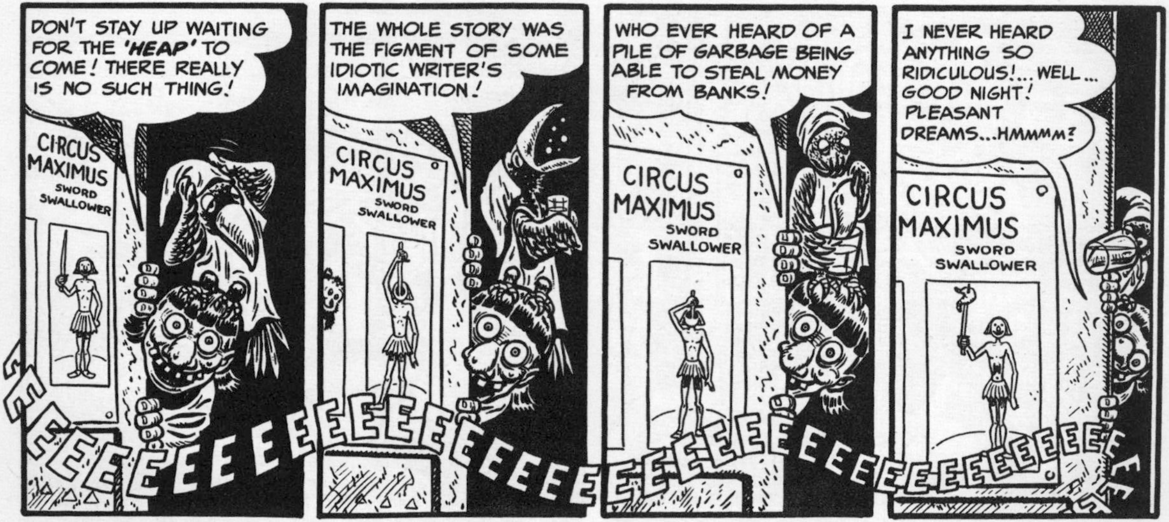
DON'T STAY UP WAITING FOR THE 'HEAP' TO COME! THERE REALLY IS NO SUCH THING!
CIRCUS MAXIMUS
SWORD SWALLOWER
THE WHOLE STORY WAS THE FIGMENT OF SOME IDIOTIC WRITER'S IMAGINATION!
CIRCUS MAXIMUS
SWORD SWALLOWER
WHO EVER HEARD OF A PILE OF GARBAGE BEING ABLE TO STEAL MONEY FROM BANKS!
CIRCUS MAXIMUS
SWORD SWALLOWER
I NEVER HEARD ANYTHING SO RIDICULOUS!... WELL... GOOD NIGHT! PLEASANT DREAMS...HMMMM?
CIRCUS MAXIMUS
SWORD SWALLOWER
EEEEEEEEEEEEEEEEEEEEEEEEEEEEEEEEEEEEEEEEEEEEE

EEEEEEEEEEEEEEEEEEEE
CLUNK!

HEY! LOOK HERE!
I FORGOT TO TAKE THE GARBAGE OUT!
WAIT A MINUTE!
IT'S NOT GARBAGE!
IT'S...
IT'S...
HEAP!

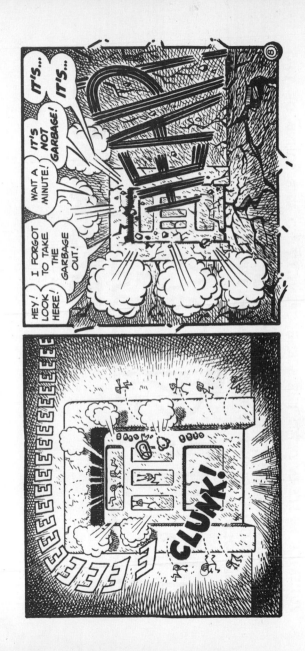

JUVENILE WESTERN DEPT: THE SCENE OPENS UP TO THE SOUND OF TWO THUNDERING SIX-GUNS . . . TO THE SOUND OF GOLDEN BULLETS TEARING THROUGH THE AIR . . . TO THE SOUND OF THE WILLIAM TELL OVERTURE IN THE BACKGROUND! OUT OF THE PAST COME THE HOOFBEATS OF THE GREAT HORSE GOLDEN! THE . . .

LONE STRANGER
RIDES AGAIN!

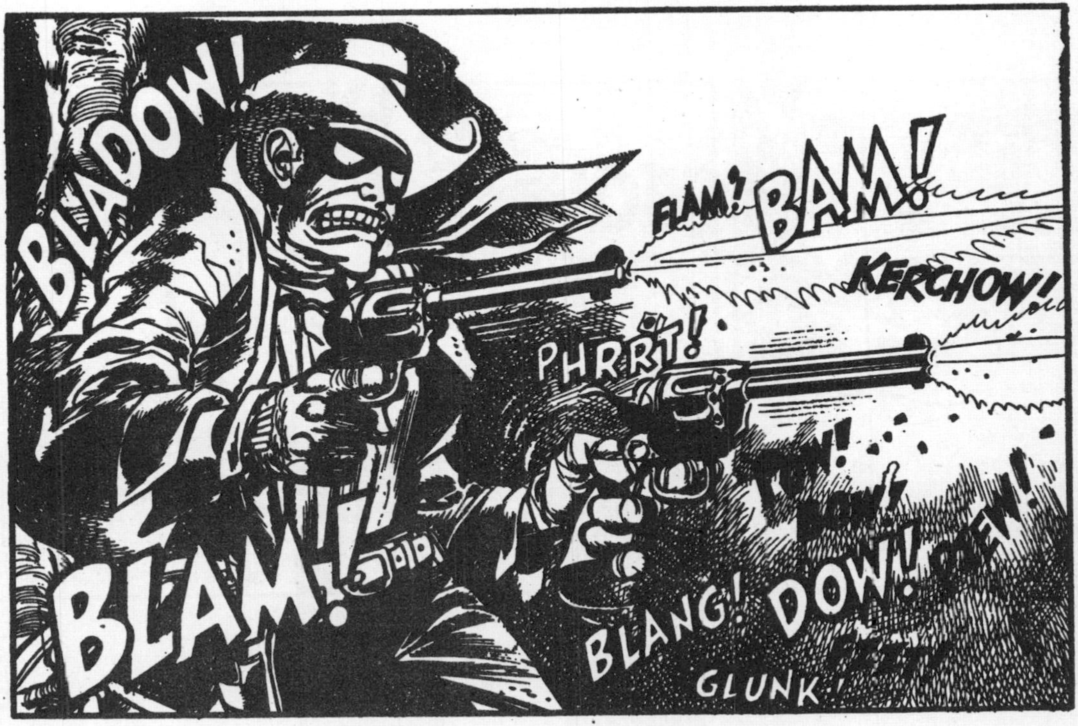
BLADOW!
FLAM! BAM!
KERCHOW!
PHRRT!
BLAM!
BLANG! DOW!
GLUNK!

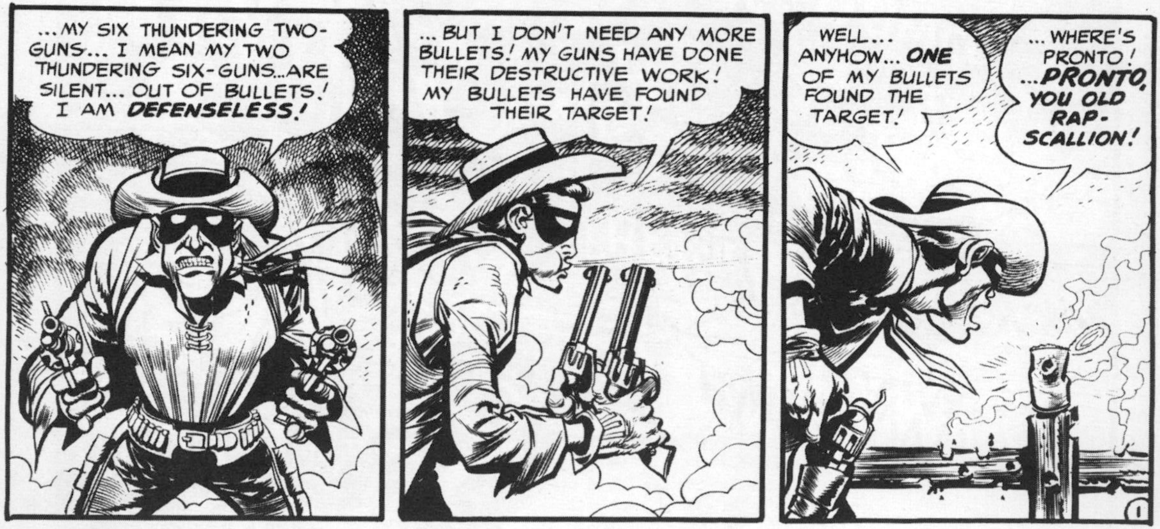
...MY SIX THUNDERING TWO-GUNS... I MEAN MY TWO THUNDERING SIX-GUNS...ARE SILENT... OUT OF BULLETS! I AM **DEFENSELESS!**
... BUT I DON'T NEED ANY MORE BULLETS! MY GUNS HAVE DONE THEIR DESTRUCTIVE WORK! MY BULLETS HAVE FOUND THEIR TARGET!
WELL... ANYHOW... **ONE** OF MY BULLETS FOUND THE TARGET!
... WHERE'S PRONTO! ...**PRONTO, YOU OLD RAP-SCALLION!**

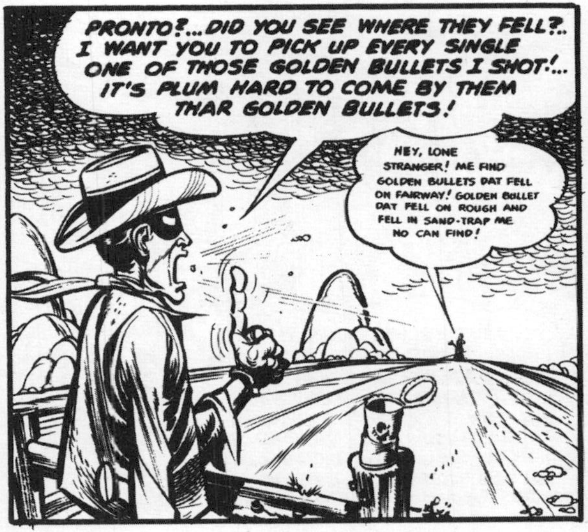
PRONTO?...DID YOU SEE WHERE THEY FELL?.. I WANT YOU TO PICK UP EVERY SINGLE ONE OF THOSE GOLDEN BULLETS I SHOT!... IT'S PLUM HARD TO COME BY THEM THAR GOLDEN BULLETS!
HEY, LONE STRANGER! ME FIND GOLDEN BULLETS DAT FELL ON FAIRWAY! GOLDEN BULLET DAT FELL ON ROUGH AND FELL IN SAND-TRAP ME NO CAN FIND!

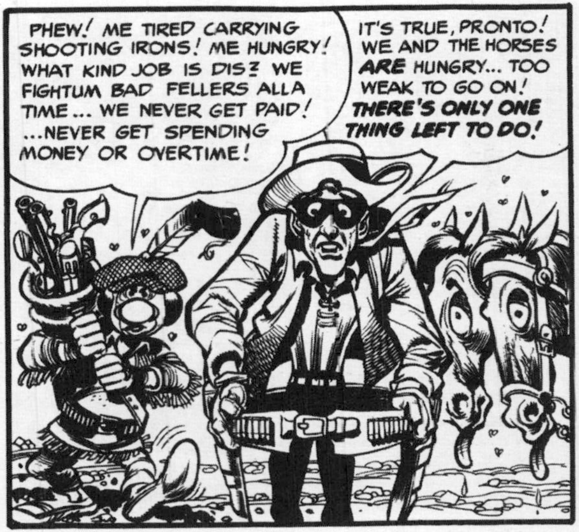
PHEW! ME TIRED CARRYING SHOOTING IRONS! ME HUNGRY! WHAT KIND JOB IS DIS? WE FIGHTUM BAD FELLERS ALLA TIME... WE NEVER GET PAID! ...NEVER GET SPENDING MONEY OR OVERTIME!
IT'S TRUE, PRONTO! WE AND THE HORSES ARE HUNGRY... TOO WEAK TO GO ON! THERE'S ONLY ONE THING LEFT TO DO!

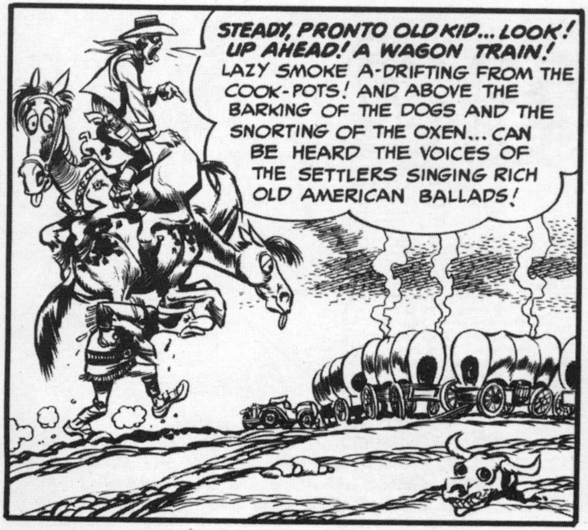
STEADY, PRONTO OLD KID... LOOK! UP AHEAD! A WAGON TRAIN! LAZY SMOKE A-DRIFTING FROM THE COOK-POTS! AND ABOVE THE BARKING OF THE DOGS AND THE SNORTING OF THE OXEN... CAN BE HEARD THE VOICES OF THE SETTLERS SINGING RICH OLD AMERICAN BALLADS!

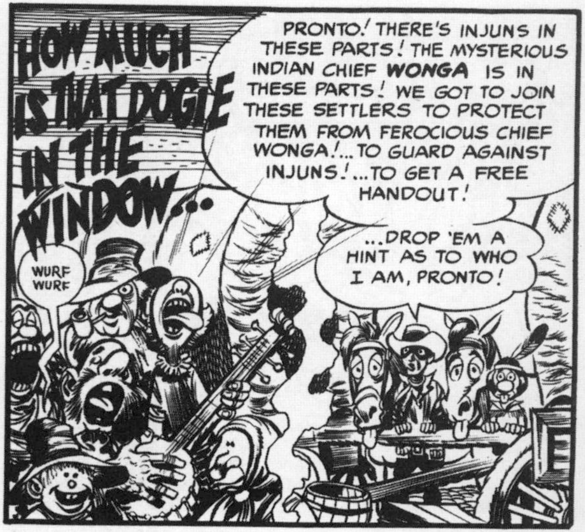
HOW MUCH IS THAT DOGIE IN THE WINDOW...
PRONTO! THERE'S INJUNS IN THESE PARTS! THE MYSTERIOUS INDIAN CHIEF **WONGA** IS IN THESE PARTS! WE GOT TO JOIN THESE SETTLERS TO PROTECT THEM FROM FEROCIOUS CHIEF WONGA!... TO GUARD AGAINST INJUNS!... TO GET A FREE HANDOUT!
WURF WURF
...DROP 'EM A HINT AS TO WHO I AM, PRONTO!

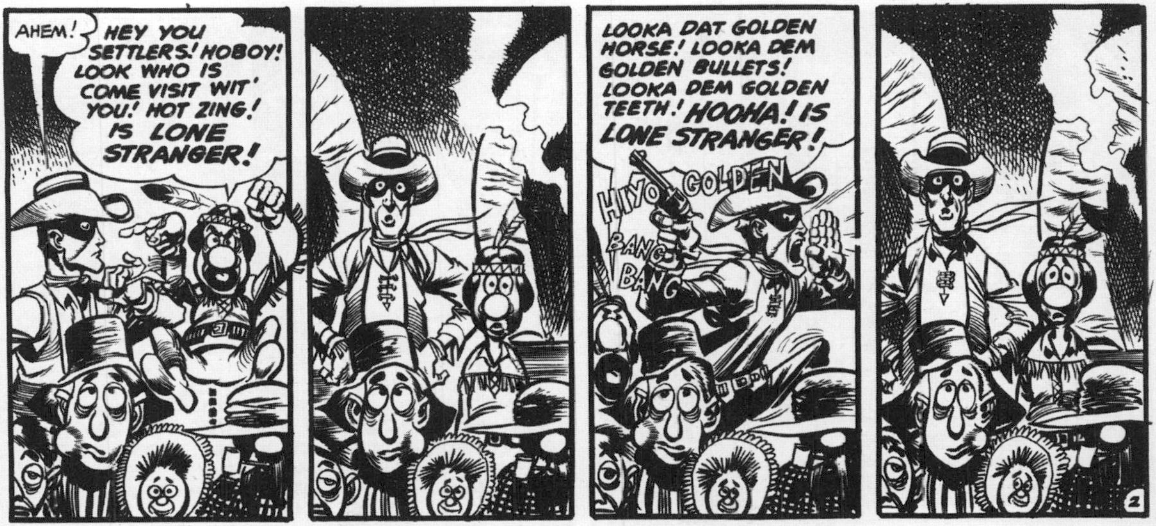
AHEM!
HEY YOU SETTLERS! HOBOY! LOOK WHO IS COME VISIT WIT' YOU! HOT ZING! IS LONE STRANGER!
LOOKA DAT GOLDEN HORSE! LOOKA DEM GOLDEN BULLETS! LOOKA DEM GOLDEN TEETH! HOOHA! IS LONE STRANGER!
HIYO GOLDEN
BANG
BANG

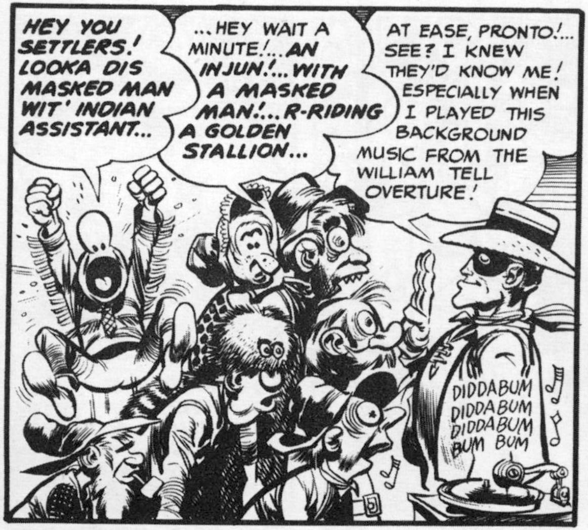
HEY YOU SETTLERS! LOOKA DIS MASKED MAN WIT' INDIAN ASSISTANT...
...HEY WAIT A MINUTE!... AN INJUN!... WITH A MASKED MAN!... R-RIDING A GOLDEN STALLION...
AT EASE, PRONTO!... SEE? I KNEW THEY'D KNOW ME! ESPECIALLY WHEN I PLAYED THIS BACKGROUND MUSIC FROM THE WILLIAM TELL OVERTURE!
DIDDABUM DIDDABUM DIDDABUM BUM BUM

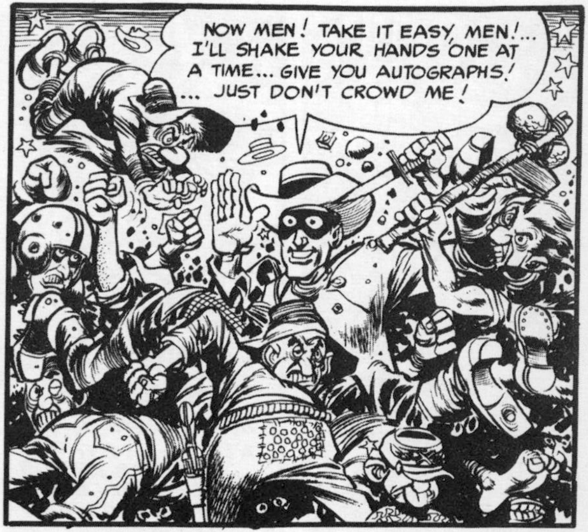
NOW MEN! TAKE IT EASY, MEN!... I'LL SHAKE YOUR HANDS ONE AT A TIME... GIVE YOU AUTOGRAPHS! ... JUST DON'T CROWD ME!

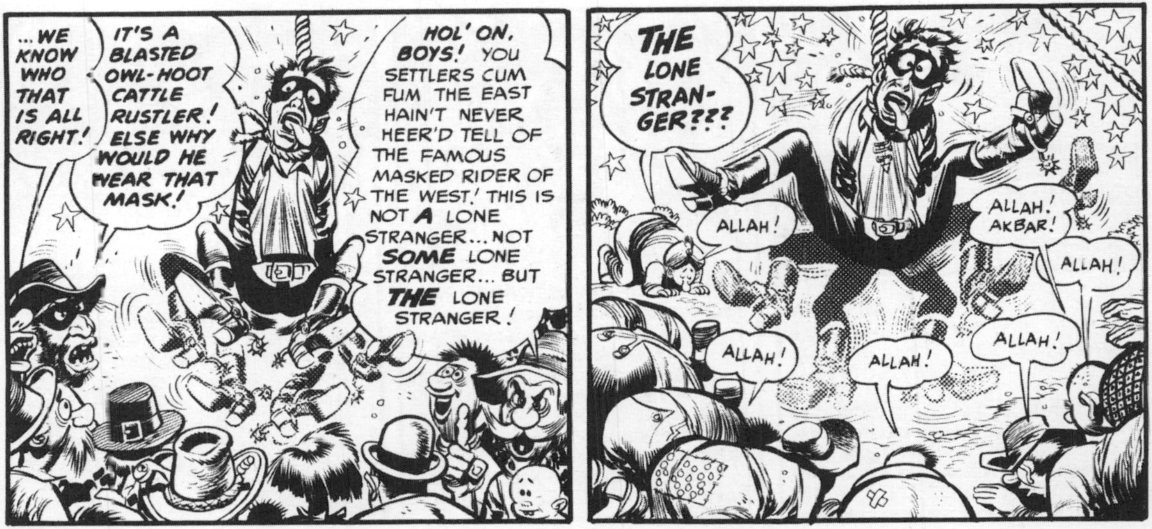
...WE KNOW WHO THAT IS ALL RIGHT!
IT'S A BLASTED OWL-HOOT CATTLE RUSTLER! ELSE WHY WOULD HE WEAR THAT MASK!
HOL' ON, BOYS! YOU SETTLERS CUM FUM THE EAST HAIN'T NEVER HEER'D TELL OF THE FAMOUS MASKED RIDER OF THE WEST! THIS IS NOT A LONE STRANGER... NOT SOME LONE STRANGER... BUT THE LONE STRANGER!
THE LONE STRANGER???
ALLAH!
ALLAH! AKBAR!
ALLAH!
ALLAH!
ALLAH!
ALLAH!

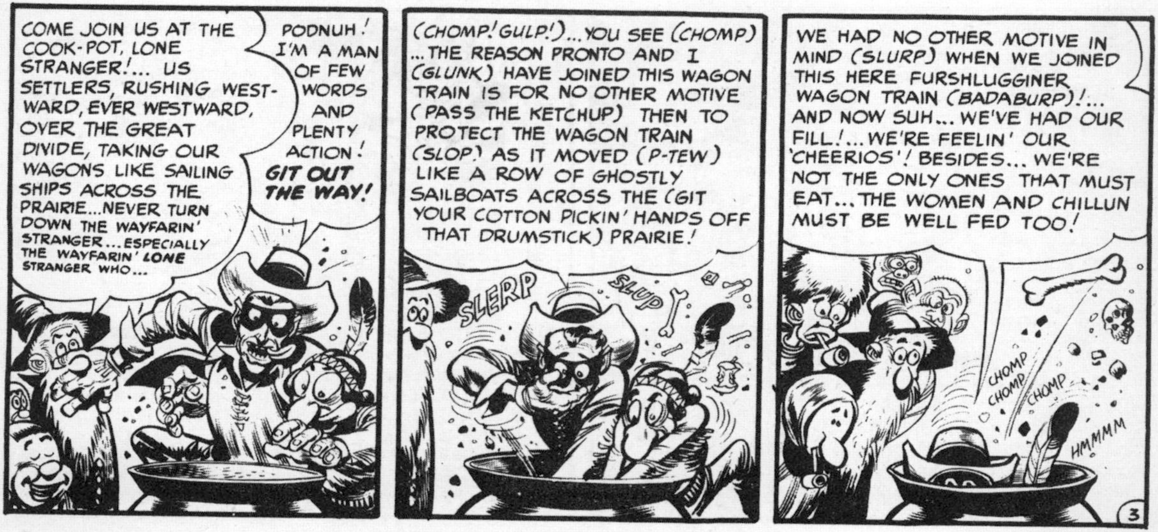

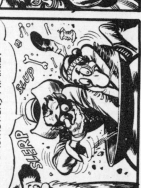

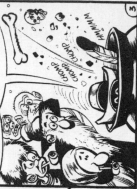

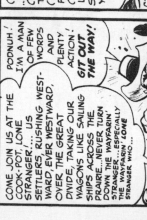

COME JOIN US AT THE COOK-POT, LONE STRANGER!... US SETTLERS, RUSHING WEST-WARD, EVER WESTWARD, OVER THE GREAT DIVIDE, TAKING OUR WAGONS LIKE SAILING SHIPS ACROSS THE PRAIRIE...NEVER TURN DOWN THE WAYFARIN' STRANGER...ESPECIALLY THE WAYFARIN' LONE STRANGER WHO...
PODNUH! I'M A MAN OF FEW WORDS AND PLENTY ACTION! GIT OUT THE WAY!
(CHOMP! GULP!)...YOU SEE (CHOMP) ...THE REASON PRONTO AND I (GLUNK) HAVE JOINED THIS WAGON TRAIN IS FOR NO OTHER MOTIVE (PASS THE KETCHUP) THEN TO PROTECT THE WAGON TRAIN (SLOP) AS IT MOVED (P-TEW) LIKE A ROW OF GHOSTLY SAILBOATS ACROSS THE (GIT YOUR COTTON PICKIN' HANDS OFF THAT DRUMSTICK) PRAIRIE!
SLERP
SLUP
WE HAD NO OTHER MOTIVE IN MIND (SLURP) WHEN WE JOINED THIS HERE FURSHLUGGINER WAGON TRAIN (BADABURP)!... AND NOW SUH... WE'VE HAD OUR FILL!...WE'RE FEELIN' OUR 'CHEERIOS'! BESIDES... WE'RE NOT THE ONLY ONES THAT MUST EAT... THE WOMEN AND CHILLUN MUST BE WELL FED TOO!
CHOMP CHOMP CHOMP
HMMMM
3

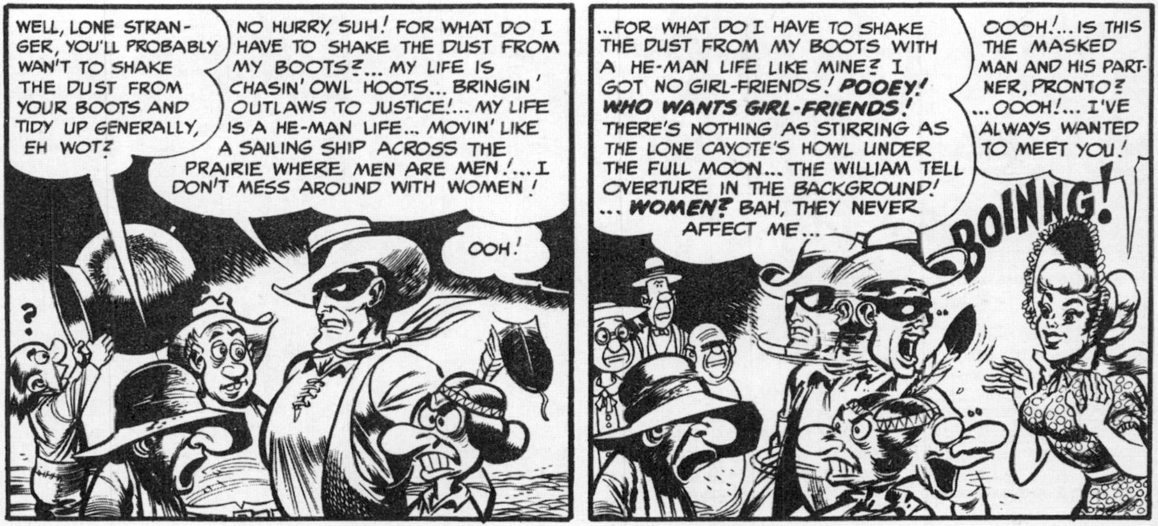
WELL, LONE STRANGER, YOU'LL PROBABLY WAN'T TO SHAKE THE DUST FROM YOUR BOOTS AND TIDY UP GENERALLY, EH WOT?
NO HURRY, SUH! FOR WHAT DO I HAVE TO SHAKE THE DUST FROM MY BOOTS?... MY LIFE IS CHASIN' OWL HOOTS... BRINGIN' OUTLAWS TO JUSTICE!... MY LIFE IS A HE-MAN LIFE... MOVIN' LIKE A SAILING SHIP ACROSS THE PRAIRIE WHERE MEN ARE MEN!... I DON'T MESS AROUND WITH WOMEN!
?
OOH!
...FOR WHAT DO I HAVE TO SHAKE THE DUST FROM MY BOOTS WITH A HE-MAN LIFE LIKE MINE? I GOT NO GIRL-FRIENDS! **POOEY! WHO WANTS GIRL-FRIENDS!** THERE'S NOTHING AS STIRRING AS THE LONE CAYOTE'S HOWL UNDER THE FULL MOON... THE WILLIAM TELL OVERTURE IN THE BACKGROUND! ... **WOMEN?** BAH, THEY NEVER AFFECT ME...
OOOH!... IS THIS THE MASKED MAN AND HIS PARTNER, PRONTO? ...OOOH!... I'VE ALWAYS WANTED TO MEET YOU!
BOINNG!

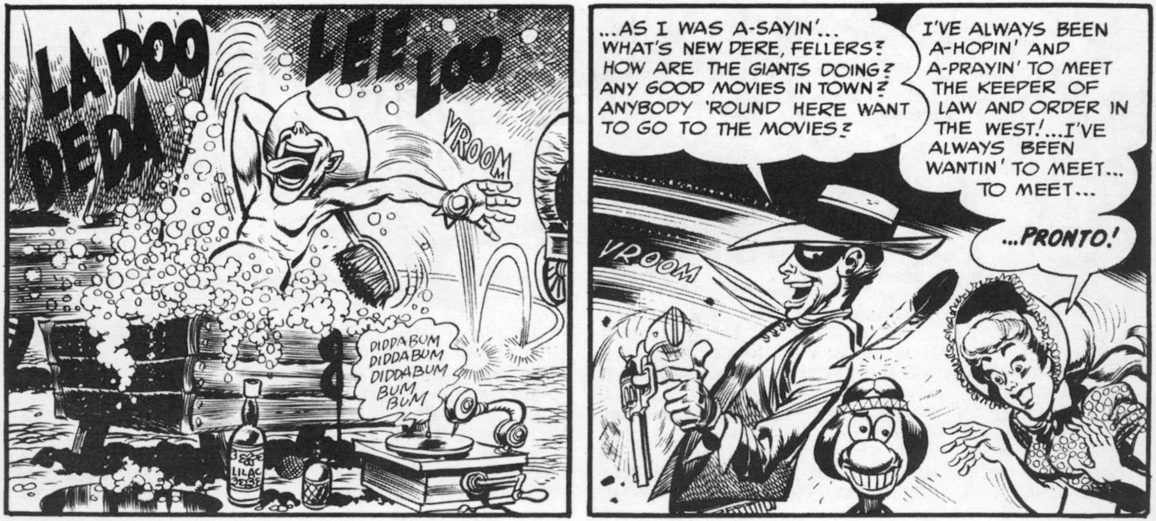
LA DOO DE DA
LEE LOO
VROOM
DIDDABUM DIDDABUM DIDDABUM BUM BUM
LILAC
...AS I WAS A-SAYIN'... WHAT'S NEW DERE, FELLERS? HOW ARE THE GIANTS DOING? ANY GOOD MOVIES IN TOWN? ANYBODY 'ROUND HERE WANT TO GO TO THE MOVIES?
I'VE ALWAYS BEEN A-HOPIN' AND A-PRAYIN' TO MEET THE KEEPER OF LAW AND ORDER IN THE WEST!...I'VE ALWAYS BEEN WANTIN' TO MEET... TO MEET...
...PRONTO!
VROOM

I HAVE A *DEFINITE* FEELING THAT THAT MYSTERIOUS CHIEF *WONGA* AND HIS TRIBE OF BLOODTHIRSTY INJUNS ARE *VERY CLOSE!* I HAVE THIS *VERY DEFINITE...* THIS *VERY VERY DEFINITE FEELING!*

THAT PRONTO IS GETTING MIGHTY UPPITY THESE DAYS!... *NOW!...* TO GET DOWN TO PROTECTING THIS WAGON TRAIN!... I HAVE A FEELING THAT INJUNS ARE *CLOSE!*

PRONTO, YOU OLD CURMUDGEON! ...*DIDN'T I TELL YOU* TO GO INTO TOWN AND LISTEN IN TO CONVERSATIONS OF FELLERS IN BARROOMS?

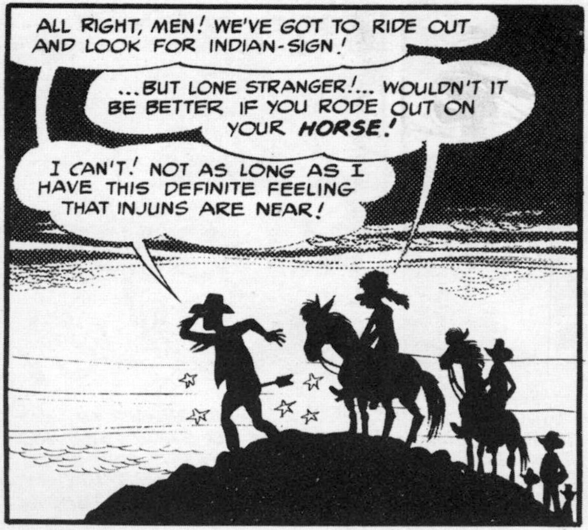
ALL RIGHT, MEN! WE'VE GOT TO RIDE OUT AND LOOK FOR INDIAN-SIGN!
...BUT LONE STRANGER!... WOULDN'T IT BE BETTER IF YOU RODE OUT ON YOUR **HORSE**!
I CAN'T! NOT AS LONG AS I HAVE THIS DEFINITE FEELING THAT INJUNS ARE NEAR!

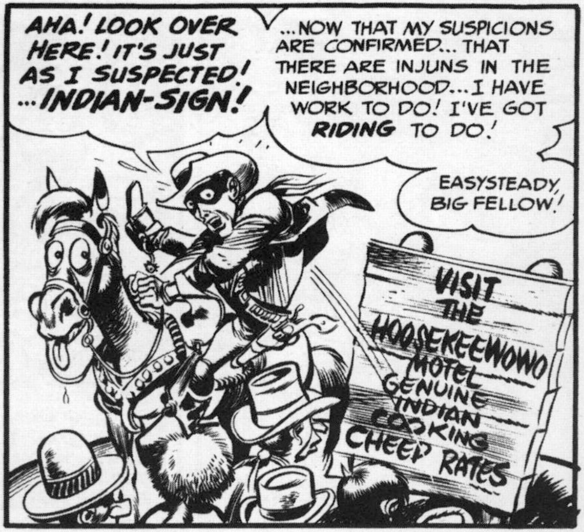
AHA! LOOK OVER HERE! IT'S JUST AS I SUSPECTED! ...INDIAN-SIGN!
...NOW THAT MY SUSPICIONS ARE CONFIRMED... THAT THERE ARE INJUNS IN THE NEIGHBORHOOD... I HAVE WORK TO DO! I'VE GOT **RIDING** TO DO!
EASYSTEADY, BIG FELLOW!
VISIT THE HOOSEKEEWOWO MOTEL GENUINE INDIAN COOKING CHEEP RATES

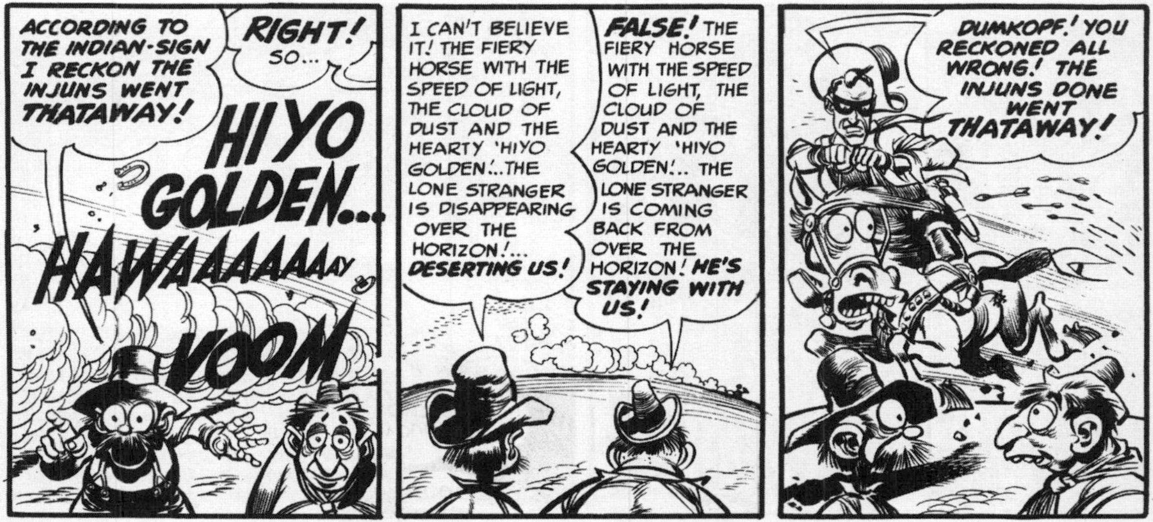
ACCORDING TO THE INDIAN-SIGN I RECKON THE INJUNS WENT THATAWAY!
RIGHT! SO...
HI YO GOLDEN... HAWAAAAAAAAY
VOOM
I CAN'T BELIEVE IT! THE FIERY HORSE WITH THE SPEED OF LIGHT, THE CLOUD OF DUST AND THE HEARTY 'HIYO GOLDEN!'...THE LONE STRANGER IS DISAPPEARING OVER THE HORIZON!... DESERTING US!
FALSE! THE FIERY HORSE WITH THE SPEED OF LIGHT, THE CLOUD OF DUST AND THE HEARTY 'HIYO GOLDEN!'... THE LONE STRANGER IS COMING BACK FROM OVER THE HORIZON! HE'S STAYING WITH US!
DUMKOPF! YOU RECKONED ALL WRONG! THE INJUNS DONE WENT THATAWAY!

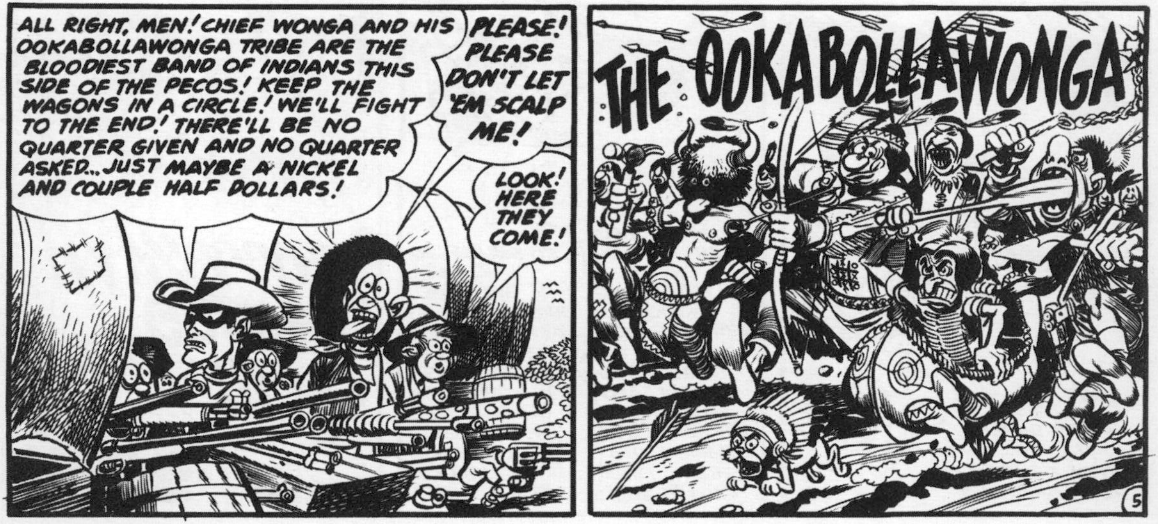
ALL RIGHT, MEN! CHIEF WONGA AND HIS OOKABOLLAWONGA TRIBE ARE THE BLOODIEST BAND OF INDIANS THIS SIDE OF THE PECOS! KEEP THE WAGONS IN A CIRCLE! WE'LL FIGHT TO THE END! THERE'LL BE NO QUARTER GIVEN AND NO QUARTER ASKED... JUST MAYBE A NICKEL AND COUPLE HALF DOLLARS!
PLEASE! PLEASE DON'T LET 'EM SCALP ME!
LOOK! HERE THEY COME!
THE OOKABOLLAWONGA
5

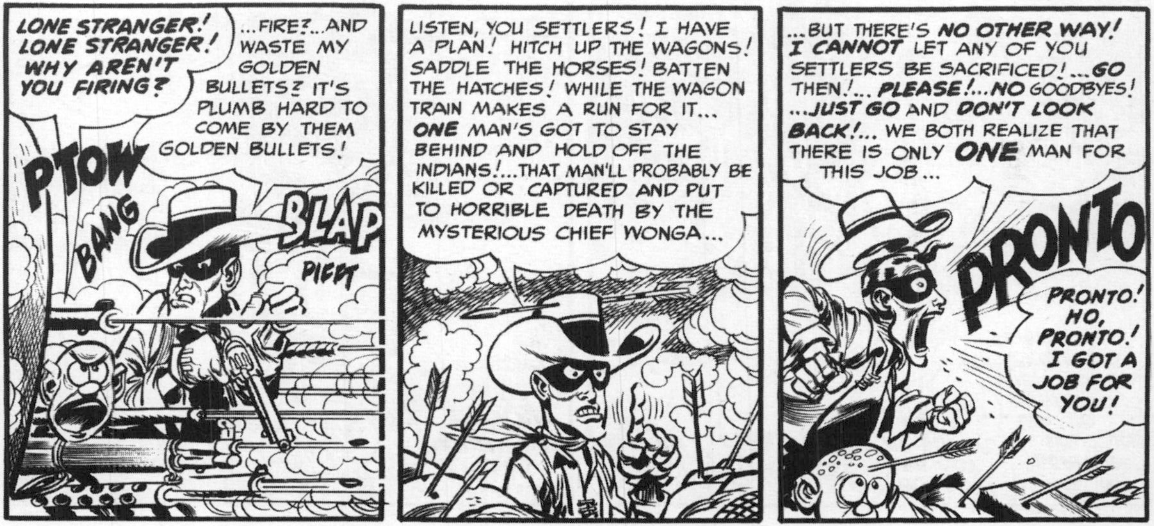
LONE STRANGER! LONE STRANGER! WHY AREN'T YOU FIRING?
...FIRE?...AND WASTE MY GOLDEN BULLETS? IT'S PLUMB HARD TO COME BY THEM GOLDEN BULLETS!
PTOW
BANG
BLAP
PICCT
LISTEN, YOU SETTLERS! I HAVE A PLAN! HITCH UP THE WAGONS! SADDLE THE HORSES! BATTEN THE HATCHES! WHILE THE WAGON TRAIN MAKES A RUN FOR IT... ONE MAN'S GOT TO STAY BEHIND AND HOLD OFF THE INDIANS!...THAT MAN'LL PROBABLY BE KILLED OR CAPTURED AND PUT TO HORRIBLE DEATH BY THE MYSTERIOUS CHIEF WONGA...
...BUT THERE'S NO OTHER WAY! I CANNOT LET ANY OF YOU SETTLERS BE SACRIFICED!...GO THEN!... PLEASE!...NO GOODBYES! ...JUST GO AND DON'T LOOK BACK!... WE BOTH REALIZE THAT THERE IS ONLY ONE MAN FOR THIS JOB...
PRONTO
PRONTO! HO, PRONTO! I GOT A JOB FOR YOU!

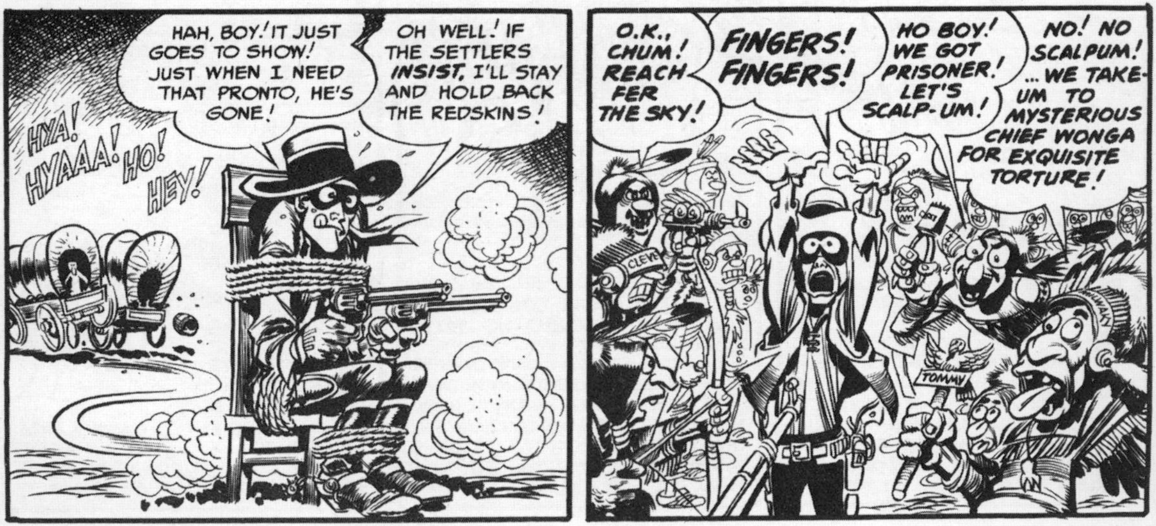
HYA! HYAAA! HO! HEY!
HAH, BOY! IT JUST GOES TO SHOW! JUST WHEN I NEED THAT PRONTO, HE'S GONE!
OH WELL! IF THE SETTLERS *INSIST*, I'LL STAY AND HOLD BACK THE REDSKINS!
O.K., CHUM! REACH FER THE SKY!
FINGERS! FINGERS!
HO BOY! WE GOT PRISONER! LET'S SCALP-UM!
NO! NO SCALPUM! ...WE TAKE-UM TO MYSTERIOUS CHIEF WONGA FOR EXQUISITE TORTURE!
CLEVE
TOMMY
MILWAKY

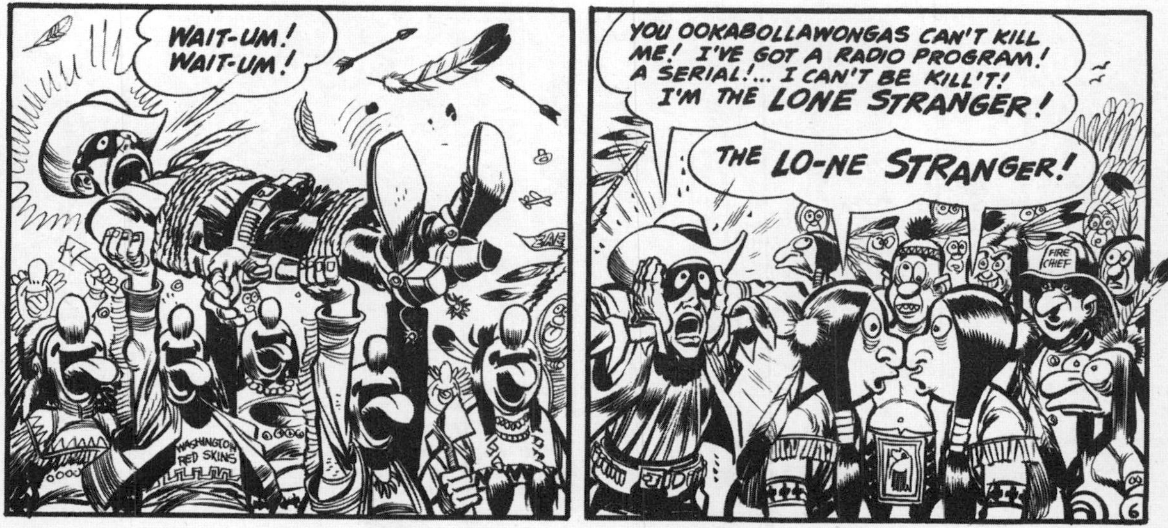
WAIT-UM!
WAIT-UM!
WASHINGTON RED SKINS
YOU OOKABOLLAWONGAS CAN'T KILL ME! I'VE GOT A RADIO PROGRAM! A SERIAL!... I CAN'T BE KILL'T! I'M THE LONE STRANGER!
THE LO-NE STRANGER!
FIRE CHIEF

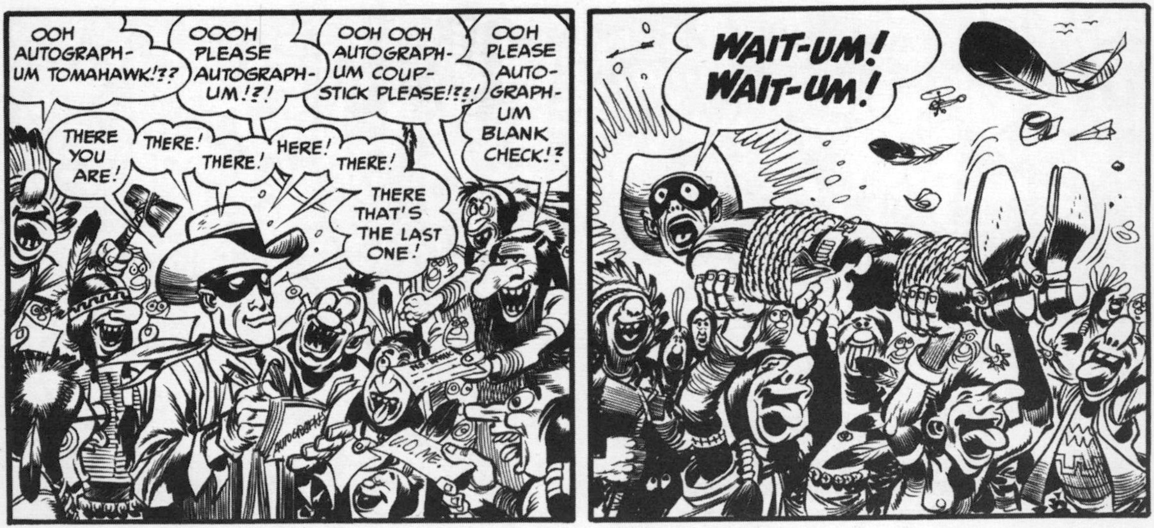
OOH AUTOGRAPH-UM TOMAHAWK!??
OOOH PLEASE AUTOGRAPH-UM!?!
OOH OOH AUTOGRAPH-UM COUP-STICK PLEASE!?!
OOH PLEASE AUTO-GRAPH-UM BLANK CHECK!?
THERE YOU ARE!
THERE!
THERE!
HERE!
THERE!
THERE THAT'S THE LAST ONE!
U.O.ME.
WAIT-UM! WAIT-UM!

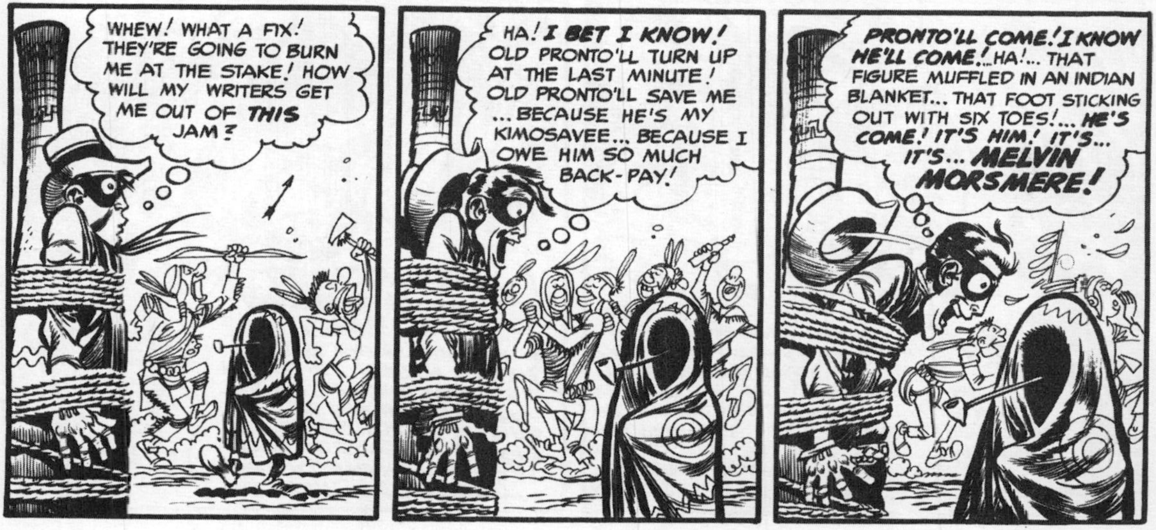
WHEW! WHAT A FIX! THEY'RE GOING TO BURN ME AT THE STAKE! HOW WILL MY WRITERS GET ME OUT OF **THIS** JAM?
HA! **I BET I KNOW!** OLD PRONTO'LL TURN UP AT THE LAST MINUTE! OLD PRONTO'LL SAVE ME ...BECAUSE HE'S MY KIMOSAVEE... BECAUSE I OWE HIM SO MUCH BACK-PAY!
PRONTO'LL COME! I KNOW HE'LL COME!...HA!... THAT FIGURE MUFFLED IN AN INDIAN BLANKET... THAT FOOT STICKING OUT WITH SIX TOES!... **HE'S COME! IT'S HIM! IT'S... IT'S... MELVIN MORSMERE!**

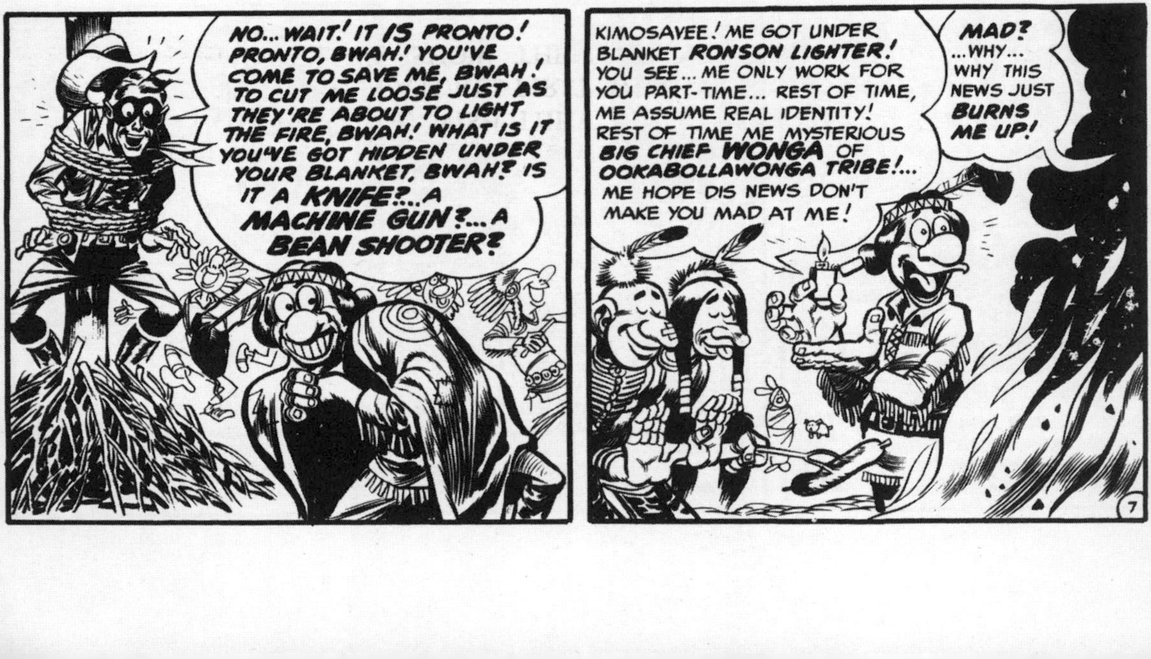
NO... WAIT! IT IS PRONTO! PRONTO, BWAH! YOU'VE COME TO SAVE ME, BWAH! TO CUT ME LOOSE JUST AS THEY'RE ABOUT TO LIGHT THE FIRE, BWAH! WHAT IS IT YOU'VE GOT HIDDEN UNDER YOUR BLANKET, BWAH? IS IT A KNIFE?... A MACHINE GUN?... A BEAN SHOOTER?
KIMOSAYEE! ME GOT UNDER BLANKET RONSON LIGHTER! YOU SEE... ME ONLY WORK FOR YOU PART-TIME... REST OF TIME, ME ASSUME REAL IDENTITY! REST OF TIME ME MYSTERIOUS BIG CHIEF WONGA OF OOKABOLLAWONGA TRIBE!... ME HOPE DIS NEWS DON'T MAKE YOU MAD AT ME!
MAD? ...WHY... WHY THIS NEWS JUST BURNS ME UP!
7

SCENES LIKE TO SEE! WE'D...

DEPT. I: SAY . . . YOU KNOW HOW IN MOVIES, T.V., ETC., YOU GET TO SEEING THE SAME IDEA . . . THE SAME SCENE . . OVER AND OVER AGAIN? . . . AND YOU KNOW HOW YOU WISH THEY DID SOMETHING DIFFERENT FOR A CHANGE? THAT'S THIS FEATURE! FIRST WE'RE GOING TO SHOW SCENES WE ALWAYS SEE! THEN WE SHOW THEM AGAIN WITH LITTLE NAUSEATING CHANGES

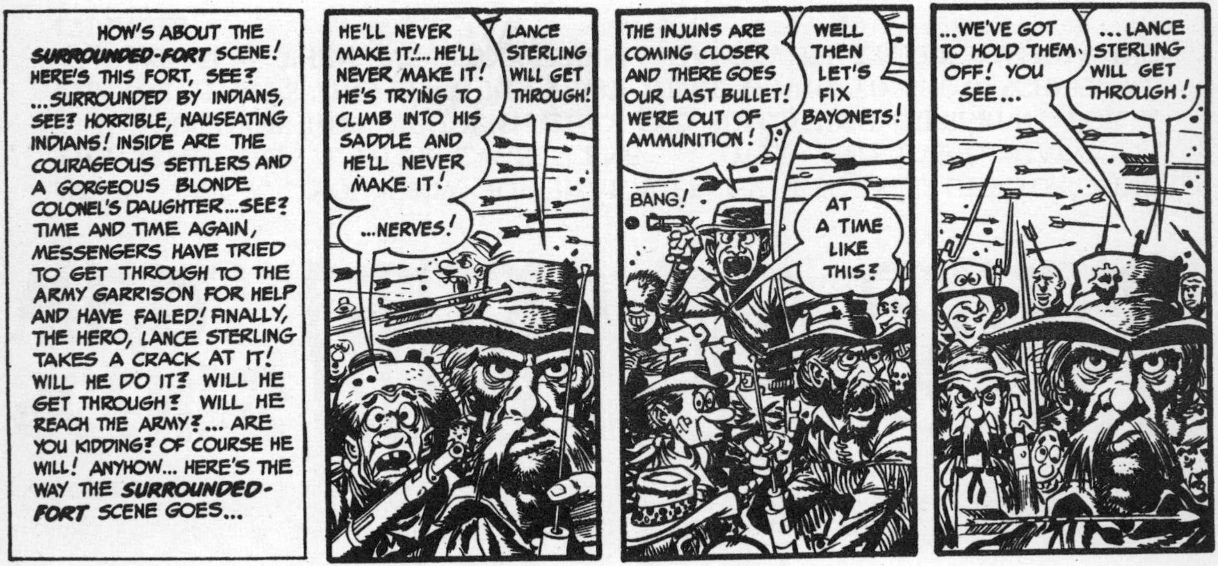
HOW'S ABOUT THE SURROUNDED-FORT SCENE! HERE'S THIS FORT, SEE? ...SURROUNDED BY INDIANS, SEE? HORRIBLE, NAUSEATING INDIANS! INSIDE ARE THE COURAGEOUS SETTLERS AND A GORGEOUS BLONDE COLONEL'S DAUGHTER...SEE? TIME AND TIME AGAIN, MESSENGERS HAVE TRIED TO GET THROUGH TO THE ARMY GARRISON FOR HELP AND HAVE FAILED! FINALLY, THE HERO, LANCE STERLING TAKES A CRACK AT IT! WILL HE DO IT? WILL HE GET THROUGH? WILL HE REACH THE ARMY?... ARE YOU KIDDING? OF COURSE HE WILL! ANYHOW... HERE'S THE WAY THE SURROUNDED-FORT SCENE GOES...
HE'LL NEVER MAKE IT!... HE'LL NEVER MAKE IT! HE'S TRYING TO CLIMB INTO HIS SADDLE AND HE'LL NEVER MAKE IT!
LANCE STERLING WILL GET THROUGH!
...NERVES!
THE INJUNS ARE COMING CLOSER AND THERE GOES OUR LAST BULLET! WE'RE OUT OF AMMUNITION!
WELL THEN LET'S FIX BAYONETS!
BANG!
AT A TIME LIKE THIS?
...WE'VE GOT TO HOLD THEM OFF! YOU SEE...
... LANCE STERLING WILL GET THROUGH!

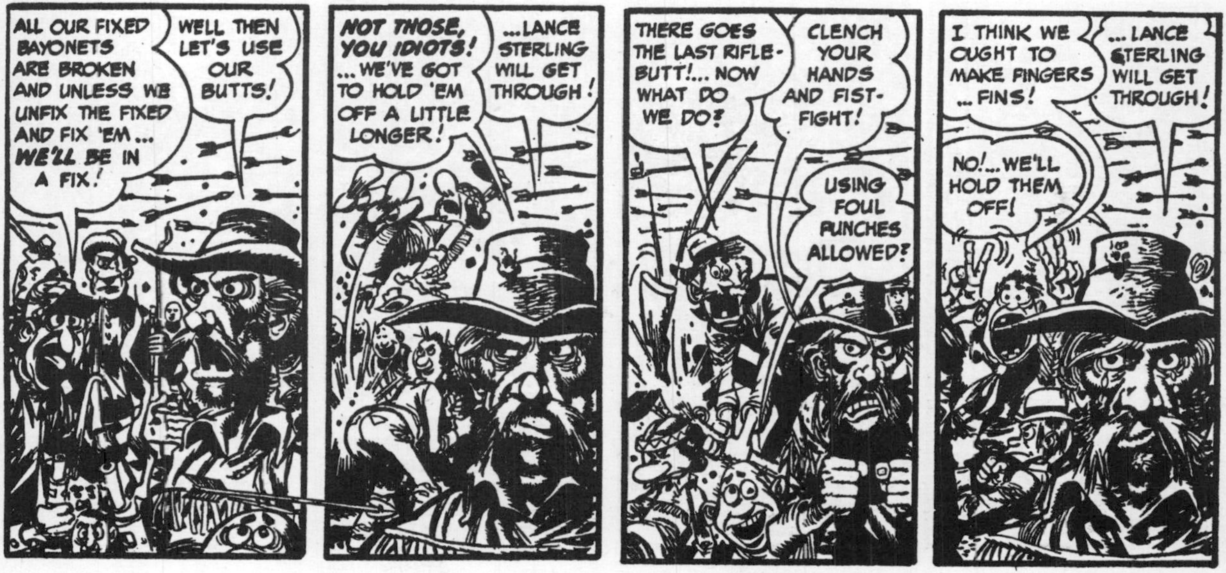
ALL OUR FIXED BAYONETS ARE BROKEN AND UNLESS WE UNFIX THE FIXED AND FIX 'EM... **WE'LL** BE IN A FIX!
WELL THEN LET'S USE OUR BUTTS!
NOT THOSE, YOU IDIOTS! ...WE'VE GOT TO HOLD 'EM OFF A LITTLE LONGER!
...LANCE STERLING WILL GET THROUGH!
THERE GOES THE LAST RIFLE-BUTT!... NOW WHAT DO WE DO?
CLENCH YOUR HANDS AND FIST-FIGHT!
USING FOUL PUNCHES ALLOWED?
I THINK WE OUGHT TO MAKE FINGERS ...FINS!
...LANCE STERLING WILL GET THROUGH!
NO!...WE'LL HOLD THEM OFF!

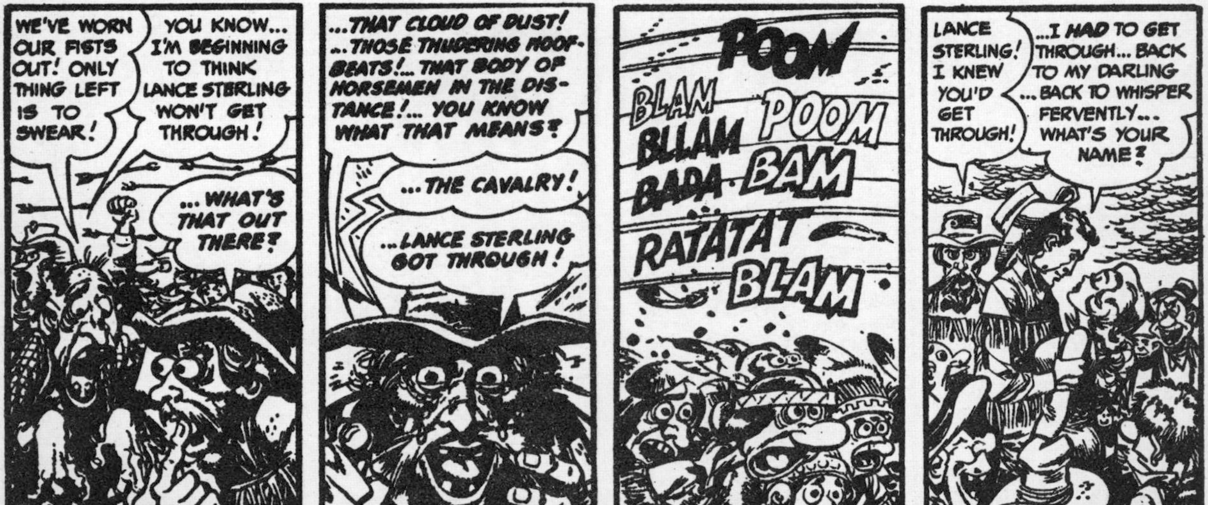
WE'VE WORN OUR FISTS OUT! ONLY THING LEFT IS TO SWEAR!
YOU KNOW... I'M BEGINNING TO THINK LANCE STERLING WON'T GET THROUGH!
...WHAT'S THAT OUT THERE?
...THAT CLOUD OF DUST! ...THOSE THUDERING HOOF-BEATS!... THAT BODY OF HORSEMEN IN THE DIS-TANCE!... YOU KNOW WHAT THAT MEANS?
...THE CAVALRY!
...LANCE STERLING GOT THROUGH!
POOM
BLAM
BLLAM
POOM
BADA BAM
RATATAT
BLAM
LANCE STERLING! I KNEW YOU'D GET THROUGH!
...I HAD TO GET THROUGH... BACK TO MY DARLING ...BACK TO WHISPER FERVENTLY... WHAT'S YOUR NAME?
4

...NOW HERE'S THE SURROUN-DED-FORT SCENE THE WAY WE'D LIKE TO SEE IT!

58

NAVY DEPT: HERE IS ONE OF THE AMAZING HERETOFORE UNTOLD STORIES IN THE ANNALS OF THE SEA. ONCE THERE WAS THIS OLD SAILOR . . . WHO GOT THIS BEAUTIFUL WALKING-STICK FOR A PRESENT . . . AND WHEN THEY ASKED HIM TO USE IT, THE OLD GOAT REBELLED! . . . AFTER ALL . . . WHO WANTS A WALKING STICK? . . . A STICK THAT STANDS STILL IS MUCH BETTER! . . . THIS, THEN, IS OUR STORY . . . THE WALKING-STICK REBELLION . . . OR . . .

THE CANE MUTINY!

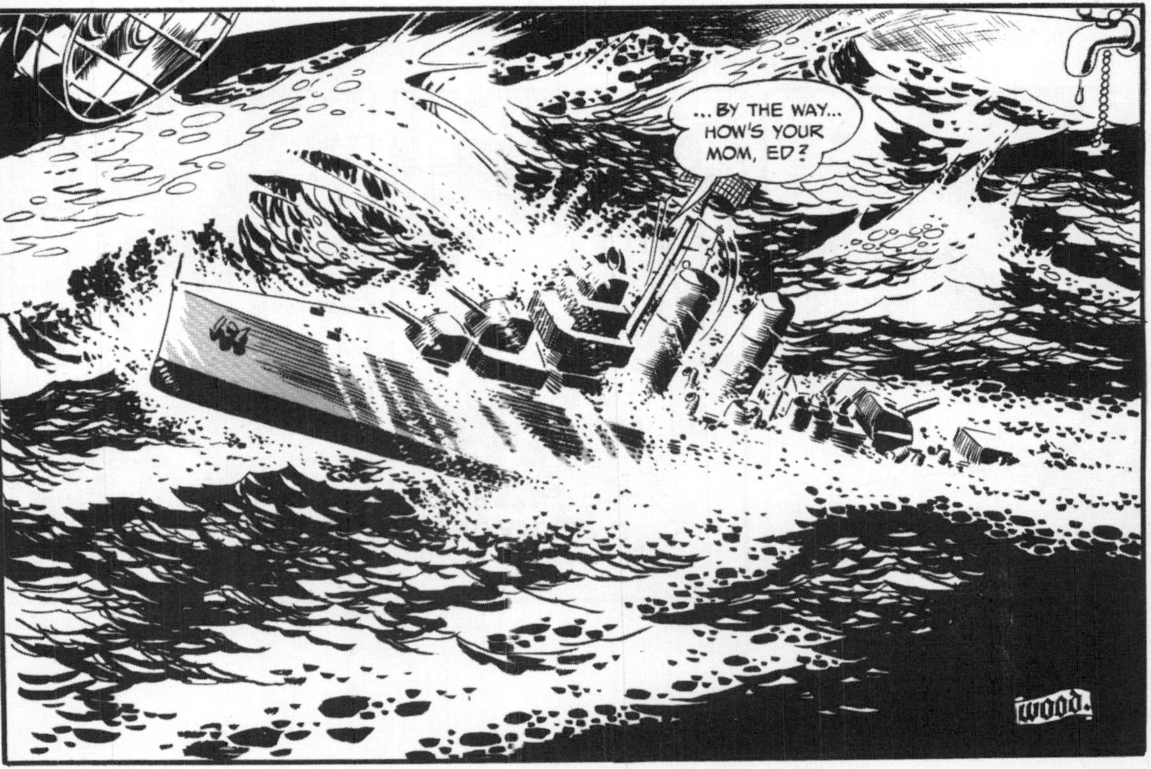
...BY THE WAY... HOW'S YOUR MOM, ED?
WOOD.

WHEE
LIFE
SAVER
...NOT THAT THIS HAS MUCH TO DO WITH MAIN STORY IDEA BUT A STORY HAS GOT TO HAVE ROMANTIC INTEREST, BY GEORGE!

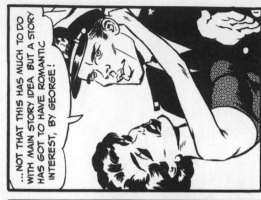

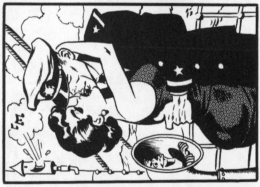

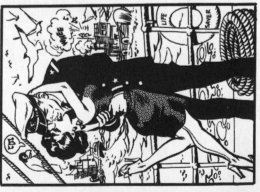

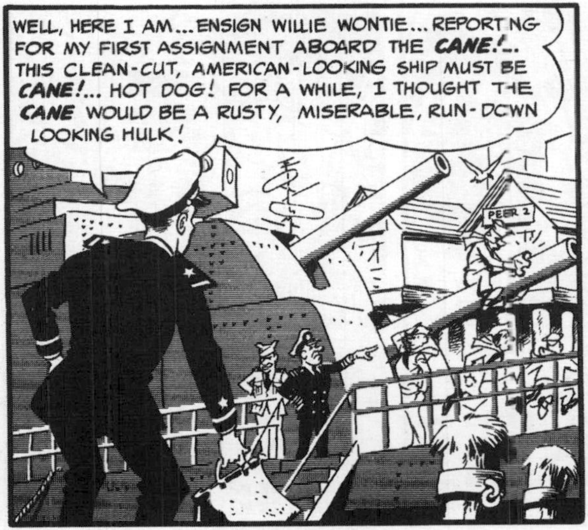
WELL, HERE I AM...ENSIGN WILLIE WONTIE...REPORTING FOR MY FIRST ASSIGNMENT ABOARD THE CANE!... THIS CLEAN-CUT, AMERICAN-LOOKING SHIP MUST BE CANE!... HOT DOG! FOR A WHILE, I THOUGHT THE CANE WOULD BE A RUSTY, MISERABLE, RUN-DOWN LOOKING HULK!
PEER 2

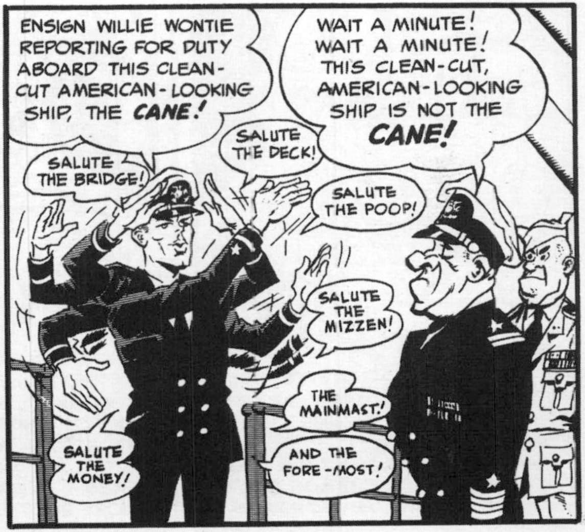
ENSIGN WILLIE WONTIE REPORTING FOR DUTY ABOARD THIS CLEAN-CUT AMERICAN-LOOKING SHIP, THE CANE!
SALUTE THE BRIDGE!
SALUTE THE DECK!
SALUTE THE POOP!
SALUTE THE MIZZEN!
THE MAINMAST!
AND THE FORE-MOST!
SALUTE THE MONEY!
WAIT A MINUTE! WAIT A MINUTE! THIS CLEAN-CUT, AMERICAN-LOOKING SHIP IS NOT THE CANE!

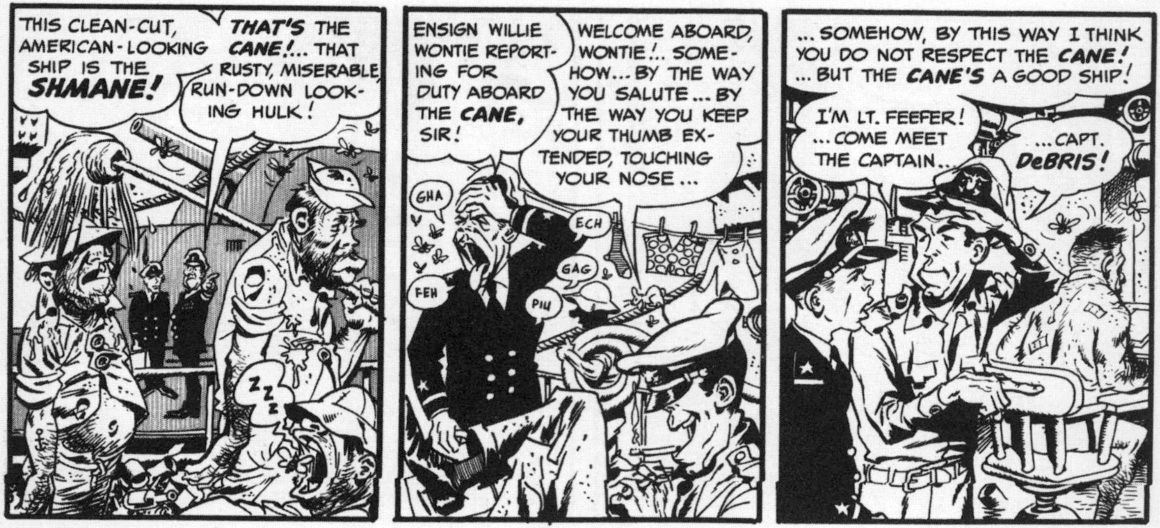
THIS CLEAN-CUT, AMERICAN-LOOKING SHIP IS THE **SHMANE!**
THAT'S THE **CANE!**... THAT RUSTY, MISERABLE, RUN-DOWN LOOKING HULK!
Z Z Z
ENSIGN WILLIE WONTIE REPORTING FOR DUTY ABOARD THE **CANE,** SIR!
WELCOME ABOARD, WONTIE!... SOMEHOW... BY THE WAY YOU SALUTE... BY THE WAY YOU KEEP YOUR THUMB EXTENDED, TOUCHING YOUR NOSE...
GHA
FEH
ECH
GAG
PIU
... SOMEHOW, BY THIS WAY I THINK YOU DO NOT RESPECT THE **CANE!** ... BUT THE **CANE'S** A GOOD SHIP!
I'M LT. FEEFER! ... COME MEET THE CAPTAIN...
... CAPT. **DeBRIS!**

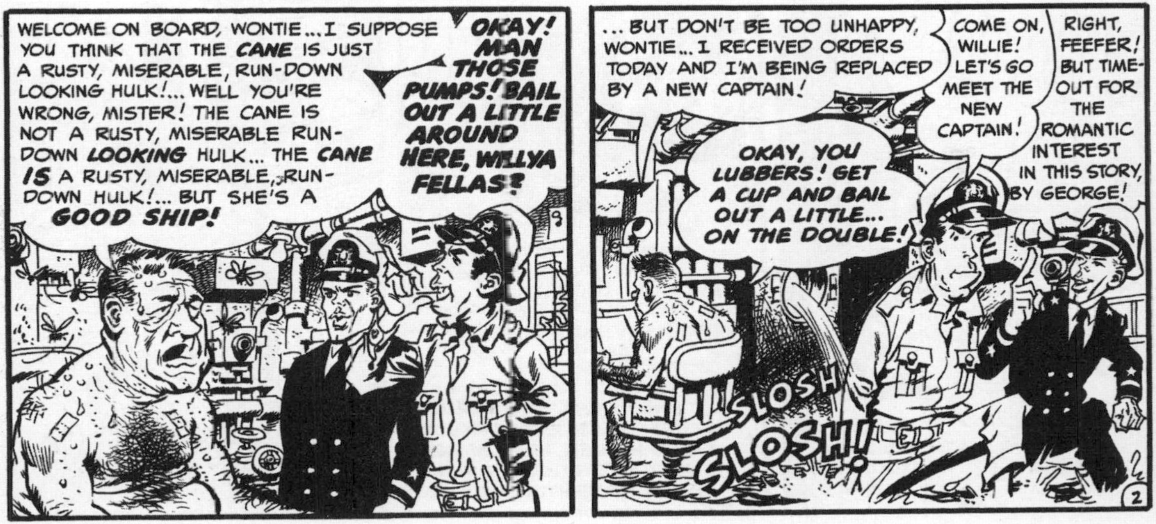
WELCOME ON BOARD, WONTIE...I SUPPOSE YOU THINK THAT THE **CANE** IS JUST A RUSTY, MISERABLE, RUN-DOWN LOOKING HULK!... WELL YOU'RE WRONG, MISTER! THE CANE IS NOT A RUSTY, MISERABLE RUN-DOWN **LOOKING** HULK... THE **CANE** **IS** A RUSTY, MISERABLE, RUN-DOWN HULK!... BUT SHE'S A **GOOD SHIP!**
OKAY! MAN THOSE PUMPS! BAIL OUT A LITTLE AROUND HERE, WILLYA FELLAS?
...BUT DON'T BE TOO UNHAPPY, WONTIE...I RECEIVED ORDERS TODAY AND I'M BEING REPLACED BY A NEW CAPTAIN!
OKAY, YOU LUBBERS! GET A CUP AND BAIL OUT A LITTLE... ON THE DOUBLE!
COME ON, WILLIE! LET'S GO MEET THE NEW CAPTAIN!
RIGHT, FEEFER! BUT TIME-OUT FOR THE ROMANTIC INTEREST IN THIS STORY, BY GEORGE!
SLOSH
SLOSH!
2

?
COME ON, WILLIE! DON'T YOU KNOW H.Q. UP AT ComServPac SENT A T.B.S. THROUGH BuPers ON THE FOX SCHED. TO REPORT TO THE O.O.D. ON THE CONN... HAH?... DON'T YOU KNOW?
CUT OUT THE ABBREVIATIONS, FEEFER!... YOU THINK THIS IS 'DRAGNET' OR SOMETHING WITH THOSE ABBREVIATIONS?
...WILLIE, I WANT YOU TO MEET THE NEW CAPTAIN...
...CAPTAIN KWEEG!

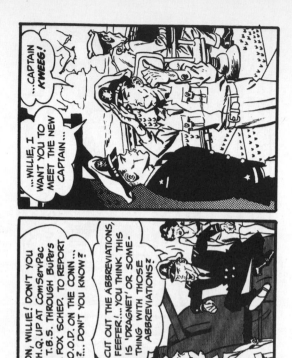

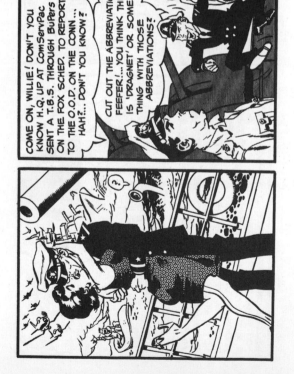

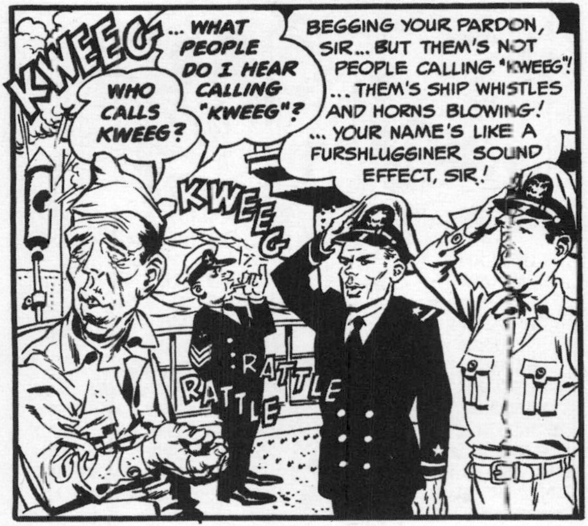
KWEEG
WHO CALLS KWEEG?
... WHAT PEOPLE DO I HEAR CALLING "KWEEG"?
KWEEG
BEGGING YOUR PARDON, SIR... BUT THEM'S NOT PEOPLE CALLING "KWEEG"! ... THEM'S SHIP WHISTLES AND HORNS BLOWING! ... YOUR NAME'S LIKE A FURSHLUGGINER SOUND EFFECT, SIR!
RATTLE RATTLE RATTLE

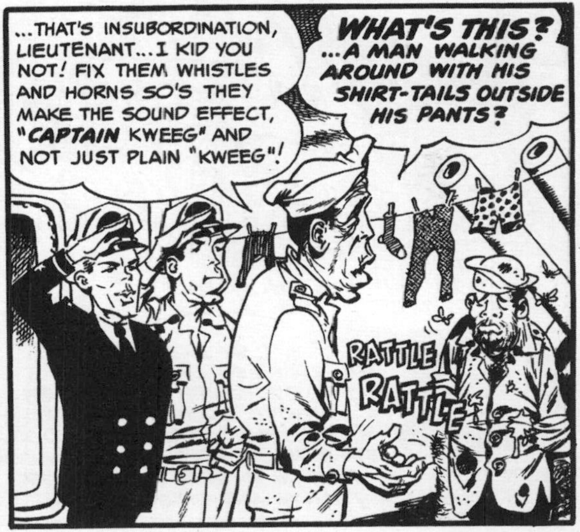
...THAT'S INSUBORDINATION, LIEUTENANT...I KID YOU NOT! FIX THEM WHISTLES AND HORNS SO'S THEY MAKE THE SOUND EFFECT, "CAPTAIN KWEEG" AND NOT JUST PLAIN "KWEEG"!
WHAT'S THIS? ...A MAN WALKING AROUND WITH HIS SHIRT-TAILS OUTSIDE HIS PANTS?
RATTLE RATTLE

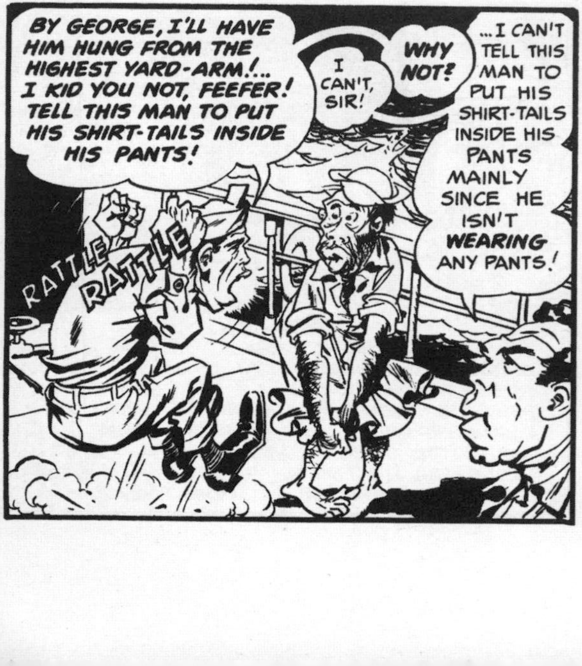
BY GEORGE, I'LL HAVE HIM HUNG FROM THE HIGHEST YARD-ARM!... I KID YOU NOT, FEEFER! TELL THIS MAN TO PUT HIS SHIRT-TAILS INSIDE HIS PANTS!
I CAN'T, SIR!
WHY NOT?
...I CAN'T TELL THIS MAN TO PUT HIS SHIRT-TAILS INSIDE HIS PANTS MAINLY SINCE HE ISN'T WEARING ANY PANTS!
RATTLE RATTLE

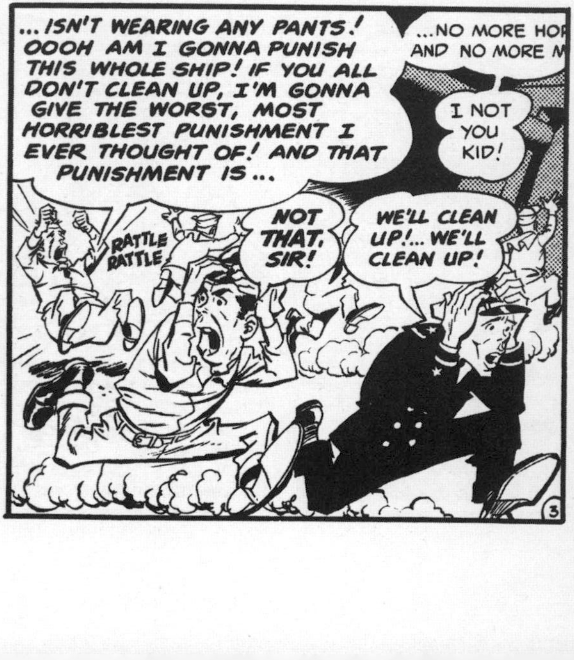
...ISN'T WEARING ANY PANTS! OOOH AM I GONNA PUNISH THIS WHOLE SHIP! IF YOU ALL DON'T CLEAN UP, I'M GONNA GIVE THE WORST, MOST HORRIBLEST PUNISHMENT I EVER THOUGHT OF! AND THAT PUNISHMENT IS...
I NOT YOU KID!
RATTLE RATTLE
NOT THAT, SIR!
WE'LL CLEAN UP!... WE'LL CLEAN UP!
3

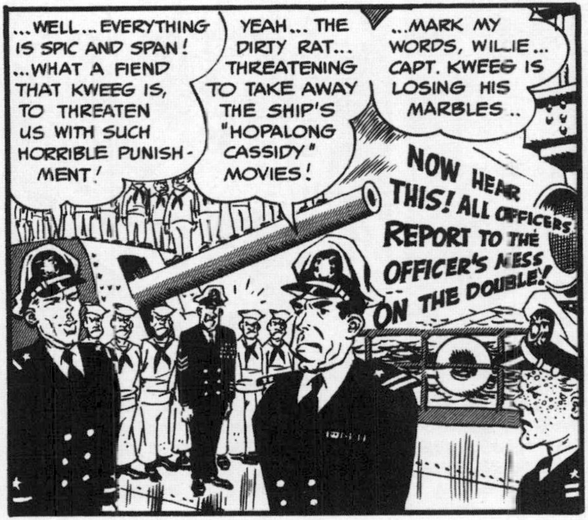
...WELL...EVERYTHING IS SPIC AND SPAN! ...WHAT A FIEND THAT KWEEG IS, TO THREATEN US WITH SUCH HORRIBLE PUNISH-MENT!
YEAH... THE DIRTY RAT... THREATENING TO TAKE AWAY THE SHIP'S "HOPALONG CASSIDY" MOVIES!
...MARK MY WORDS, WILLIE... CAPT. KWEEG IS LOSING HIS MARBLES...
NOW HEAR THIS! ALL OFFICERS REPORT TO THE OFFICER'S MESS ON THE DOUBLE!

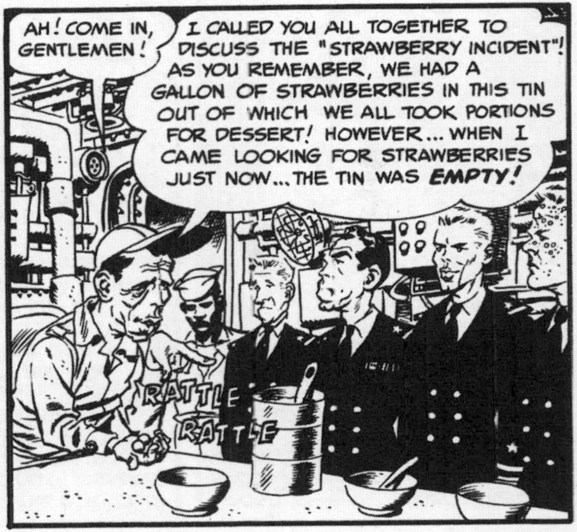
AH! COME IN, GENTLEMEN!
I CALLED YOU ALL TOGETHER TO DISCUSS THE "STRAWBERRY INCIDENT"! AS YOU REMEMBER, WE HAD A GALLON OF STRAWBERRIES IN THIS TIN OUT OF WHICH WE ALL TOOK PORTIONS FOR DESSERT! HOWEVER... WHEN I CAME LOOKING FOR STRAWBERRIES JUST NOW... THE TIN WAS *EMPTY!*
RATTLE
RATTLE

...DON'T BE RIDICULOUS! I MERELY BROUGHT YOU DOWN HERE TO ASK YOU TO JOIN ME IN A DISH OF SAND! ...UMMM YUMMY! THERE'S NOTHING I LIKE BETTER THAN A DISH OF NICE WHITE SAND!

KID I YOU NOT!

...THERE, NOW... ALL THE PORTIONS HAVE BEEN DOLED OUT! ...OBSERVE, GENTLEMEN ...THE TIN STILL HAS A *QUART* OF SAND LEFT IN IT! ...YOU KNOW WHAT THAT MEANS!

SIR! DID YOU BRING US DOWN HERE TO ACCUSE ONE OF US OF STEALING A QUART OF STRAWBERRIES?

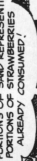

...NOW TO PROVE THAT THE TIN SHOULDN'T HAVE BEEN EMPTY, I HAVE FILLED IT WITH SAND AND THE MESS-BOY SHALL NOW DOLE OUT PORTIONS OF SAND REPRESENTING PORTIONS OF STRAWBERRIES ALREADY CONSUMED!

RATTLE RATTLE

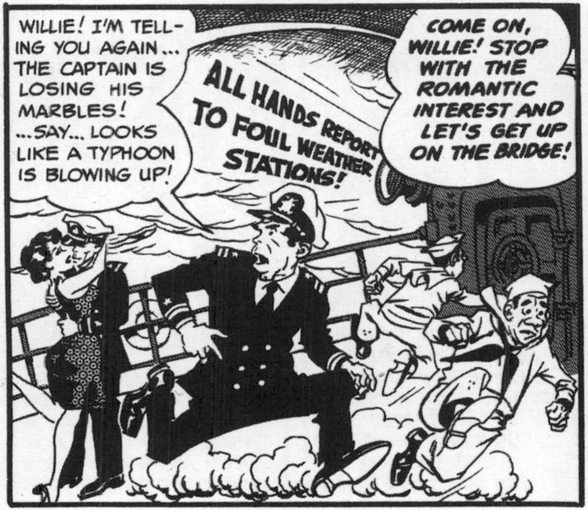
WILLIE! I'M TELLING YOU AGAIN... THE CAPTAIN IS LOSING HIS MARBLES! ...SAY... LOOKS LIKE A TYPHOON IS BLOWING UP!
ALL HANDS REPORT TO FOUL WEATHER STATIONS!
COME ON, WILLIE! STOP WITH THE ROMANTIC INTEREST AND LET'S GET UP ON THE BRIDGE!

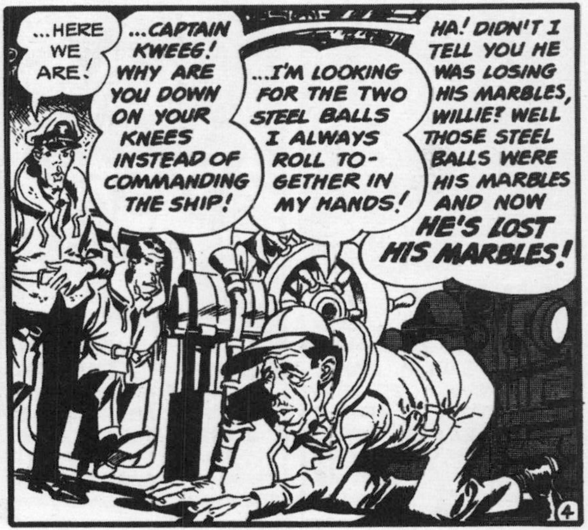
...HERE WE ARE!
...CAPTAIN KWEEG! WHY ARE YOU DOWN ON YOUR KNEES INSTEAD OF COMMANDING THE SHIP!
...I'M LOOKING FOR THE TWO STEEL BALLS I ALWAYS ROLL TOGETHER IN MY HANDS!
HA! DIDN'T I TELL YOU HE WAS LOSING HIS MARBLES, WILLIE? WELL THOSE STEEL BALLS WERE HIS MARBLES AND NOW HE'S LOST HIS MARBLES!
4

VAN!... YOU'RE SECOND IN COMMAND, VAN! CAN'T YOU SEE THE CAPTAIN'S A PARANOIA? YOU'VE GOT TO MUTINY, VAN! GET MOVING, VAN!
COFF
VAN!... CAN'T YOU SEE HIS ORDERS ARE BATTENING THE HATCH AND MESSIN' UP THE MIZZENMAST? BEFORE IT'S TOO LATE, YOU'VE GOT TO MUTINY! GET MOVING, VAN!
GLUB
VAN! CAN'T YOU SEE THE PORT-SIDE FLUGLE IS BENT AND THE SHIP CAN GET INTO SERIOUS TROUBLE? GET MOVING, VAN!
WOULDN'T A SMALL TRUCK SERVE AS WELL AS A MOVING VAN?
BURBLE
SOMEHOW BY LOOKS OF FISH SWIMMING BY MY NOSE... I THINK YOU'RE RIGHT, FEEFER!
...I HEREBY MUTINY 'CAUSE CAP-TAIN IS CRAZY, BUT MAINLY 'CAUSE TITLE OF STORY IS 'CANE MUTINY'!
BLUG

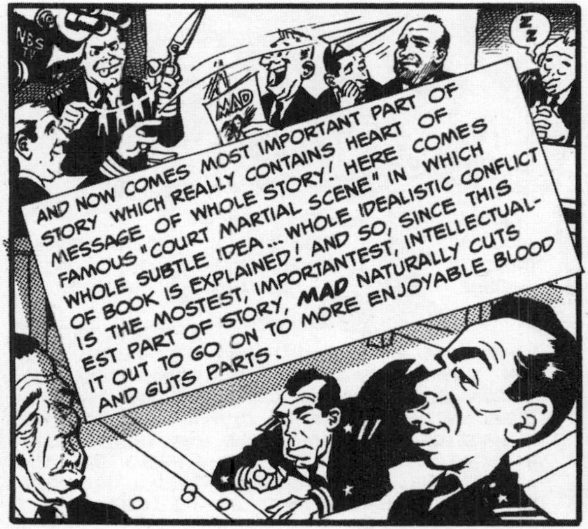
NBS TV
AND NOW COMES MOST IMPORTANT PART OF STORY WHICH REALLY CONTAINS HEART OF MESSAGE OF WHOLE STORY! HERE COMES FAMOUS "COURT MARTIAL SCENE" IN WHICH WHOLE SUBTLE IDEA... WHOLE IDEALISTIC CONFLICT OF BOOK IS EXPLAINED! AND SO, SINCE THIS IS THE MOSTEST, IMPORTANTEST, INTELLECTUAL-EST PART OF STORY, MAD NATURALLY CUTS IT OUT TO GO ON TO MORE ENJOYABLE BLOOD AND GUTS PARTS.
ZZ

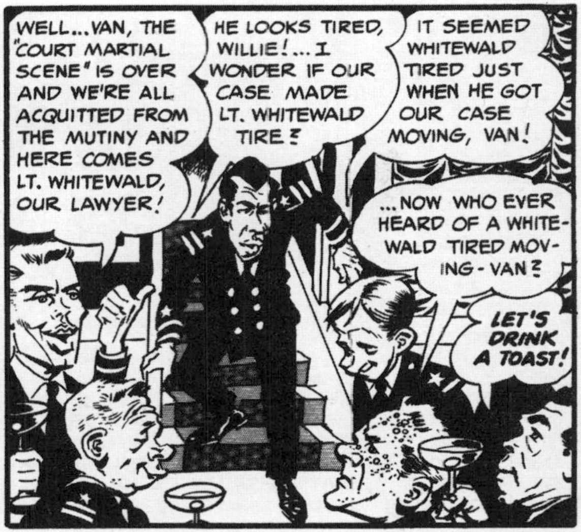
WELL...VAN, THE "COURT MARTIAL SCENE" IS OVER AND WE'RE ALL ACQUITTED FROM THE MUTINY AND HERE COMES LT. WHITEWALD, OUR LAWYER!
HE LOOKS TIRED, WILLIE!... I WONDER IF OUR CASE MADE LT. WHITEWALD TIRE?
IT SEEMED WHITEWALD TIRED JUST WHEN HE GOT OUR CASE MOVING, VAN!
...NOW WHO EVER HEARD OF A WHITE-WALD TIRED MOV-ING-VAN?
LET'S DRINK A TOAST!

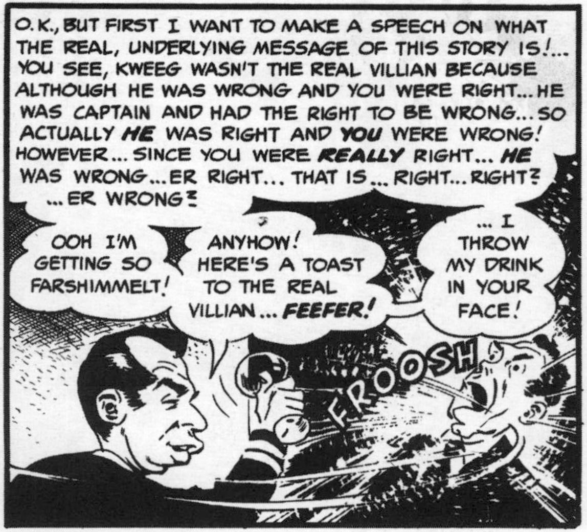
O.K., BUT FIRST I WANT TO MAKE A SPEECH ON WHAT THE REAL, UNDERLYING MESSAGE OF THIS STORY IS!... YOU SEE, KWEEG WASN'T THE REAL VILLIAN BECAUSE ALTHOUGH HE WAS WRONG AND YOU WERE RIGHT... HE WAS CAPTAIN AND HAD THE RIGHT TO BE WRONG... SO ACTUALLY HE WAS RIGHT AND YOU WERE WRONG! HOWEVER... SINCE YOU WERE REALLY RIGHT... HE WAS WRONG... ER RIGHT... THAT IS... RIGHT... RIGHT? ...ER WRONG?
OOH I'M GETTING SO FARSHIMMELT!
ANYHOW! HERE'S A TOAST TO THE REAL VILLIAN... FEEFER!
... I THROW MY DRINK IN YOUR FACE!
FROOSH

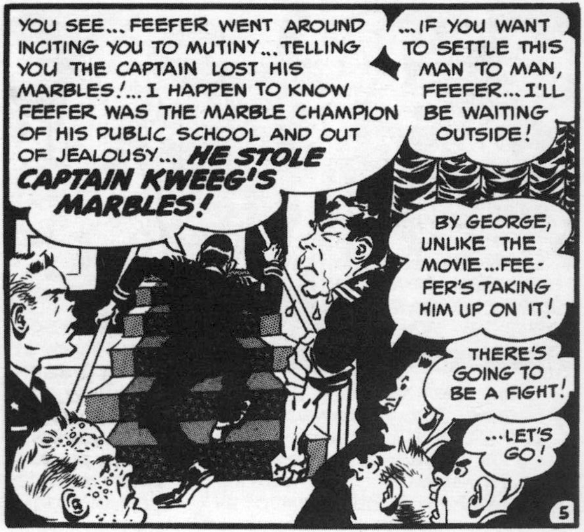
YOU SEE... FEEFER WENT AROUND INCITING YOU TO MUTINY... TELLING YOU THE CAPTAIN LOST HIS MARBLES!... I HAPPEN TO KNOW FEEFER WAS THE MARBLE CHAMPION OF HIS PUBLIC SCHOOL AND OUT OF JEALOUSY... HE STOLE CAPTAIN KWEEG'S MARBLES!
...IF YOU WANT TO SETTLE THIS MAN TO MAN, FEEFER... I'LL BE WAITING OUTSIDE!
BY GEORGE, UNLIKE THE MOVIE... FEE-FER'S TAKING HIM UP ON IT!
THERE'S GOING TO BE A FIGHT!
...LET'S GO!
5

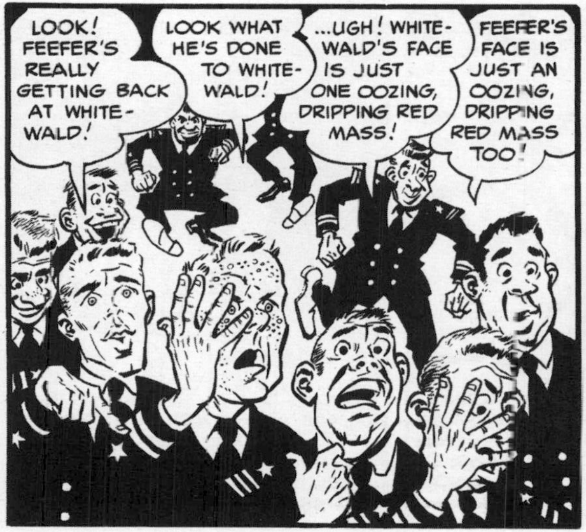
LOOK! FEEFER'S REALLY GETTING BACK AT WHITE-WALD!
LOOK WHAT HE'S DONE TO WHITE-WALD!
...UGH! WHITE-WALD'S FACE IS JUST ONE OOZING, DRIPPING RED MASS!
FEEFER'S FACE IS JUST AN OOZING, DRIPPING RED MASS TOO!

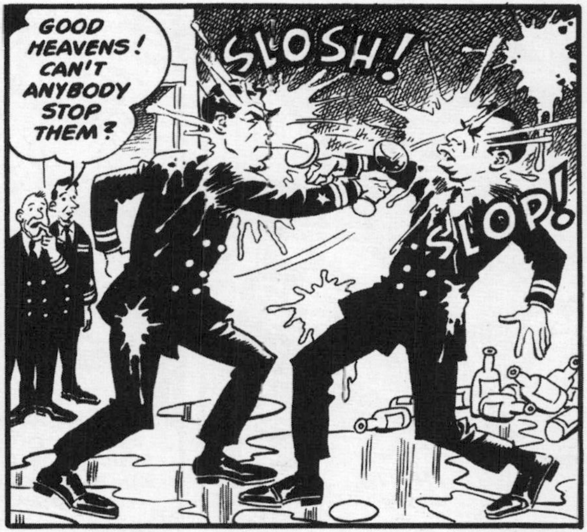
GOOD HEAVENS! CAN'T ANYBODY STOP THEM?
SLOSH!
SLOP!

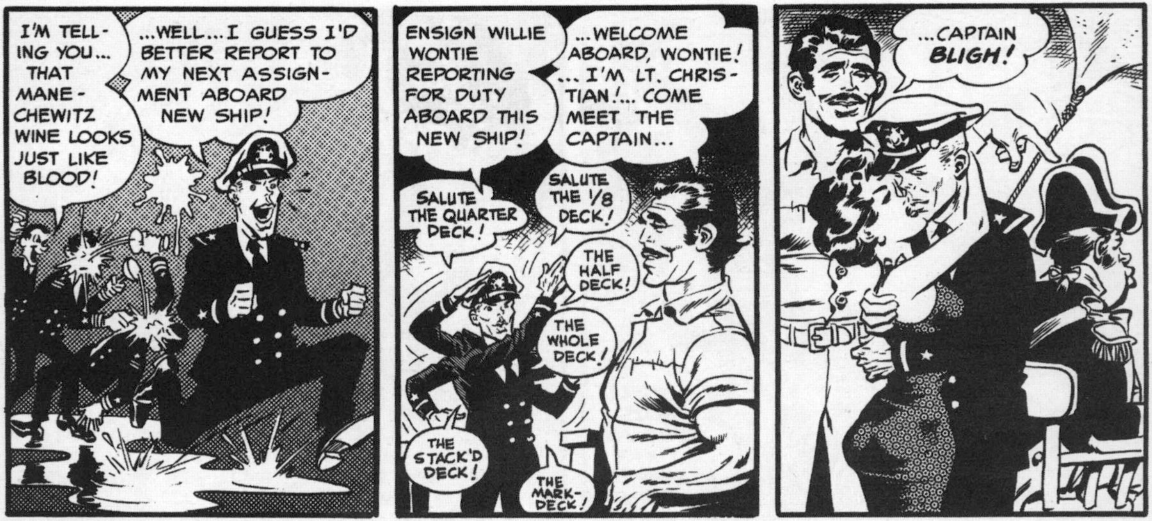
I'M TELLING YOU... THAT MANE-CHEWITZ WINE LOOKS JUST LIKE BLOOD!
...WELL... I GUESS I'D BETTER REPORT TO MY NEXT ASSIGNMENT ABOARD NEW SHIP!
ENSIGN WILLIE WONTIE REPORTING FOR DUTY ABOARD THIS NEW SHIP!
...WELCOME ABOARD, WONTIE! ... I'M LT. CHRISTIAN!... COME MEET THE CAPTAIN...
SALUTE THE QUARTER DECK!
SALUTE THE 1/8 DECK!
THE HALF DECK!
THE WHOLE DECK!
THE STACK'D DECK!
THE MARK-DECK!
...CAPTAIN BLIGH!

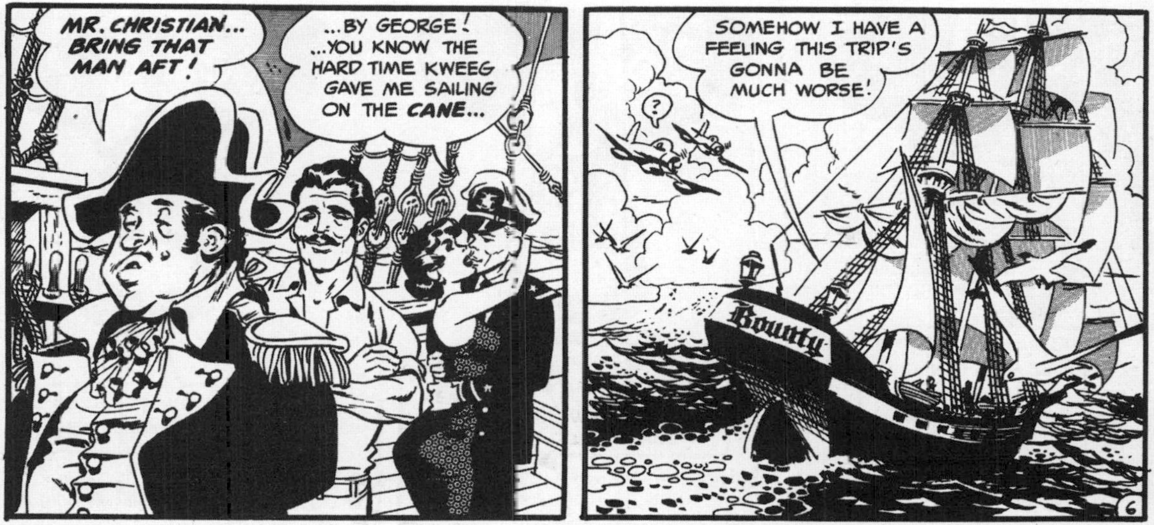
MR. CHRISTIAN... BRING THAT MAN AFT!
...BY GEORGE! ...YOU KNOW THE HARD TIME KWEEG GAVE ME SAILING ON THE CANE...
?
SOMEHOW I HAVE A FEELING THIS TRIP'S GONNA BE MUCH WORSE!
Bounty
6

TV DEPT.

I'm Konrad Strainer, Doctor of Medicine.

Tonight's case in point... Lance Follicle. Object in point... a pointy object with a case inside the point

Our story concerns a man who needed an operation... and this instrument (well known to us in the medical profession) which is a...

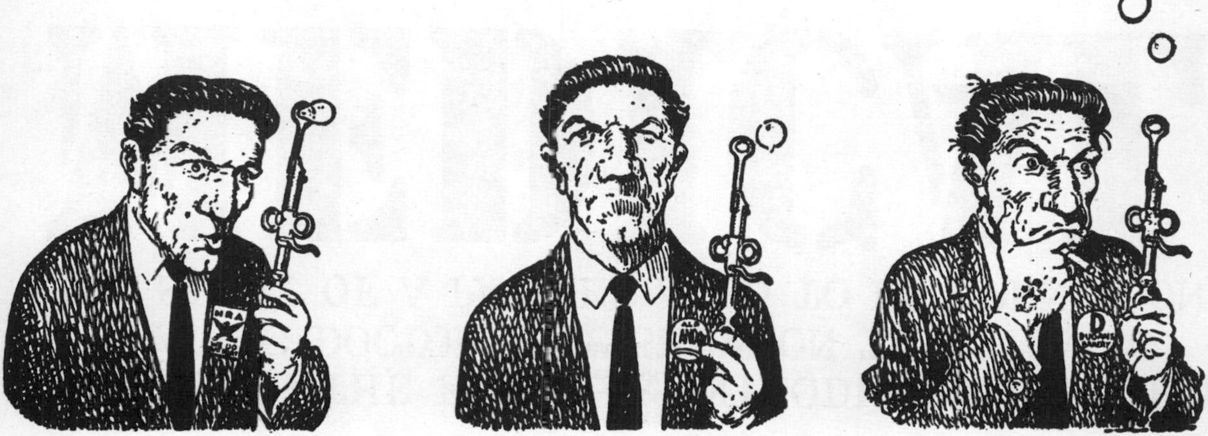
NRA
LANDON

SO BEGINS THE FAMILIAR INTRODUCTION OF THE
LEADING DOCTOR TYPE SHOW ON T.V., OPENING
THE STORY OF A PATIENT ALSO TO BE OPENED ON

MEDICAL

Yes . . . BEDSIDE MAD reviews a T.V. program that never fails to create a stir, especially when the operation scenes go on and thousands of viewers madly scramble out of the room while other thousands madly scramble into the room.

What we want to know is, are these scenes necessary? Why can't the producers eliminate these operating-room and laboratory scenes? Why can't they get rid of this technical stuff? Why do they have to be trouble-makers by sticking in educational material?

Take a tip from us, producers, and stick with good, wholesome romantic stories and stop trying to make the natives restless.

In any case, MEDICAL does manage to be exciting despite the technical material. If you watch carefully, you will notice how MEDICAL skillfully changes a commonplace sickness into a tense drama. The following pages illustrate our point. First we'll show how a sickness usually happens, and then we'll show how MEDICAL handles it.

First, in real life, here's the way a man might go off to the

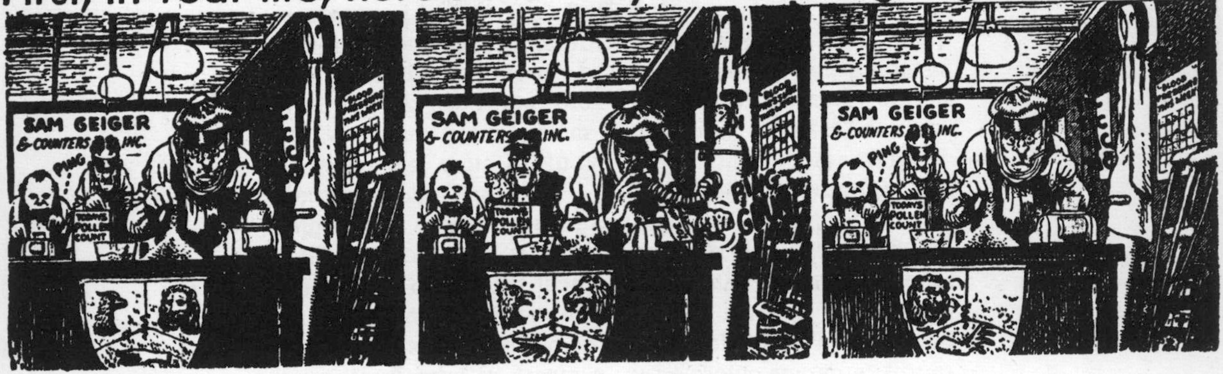
SAM GEIGER
& COUNTERS INC.
PING
TODAY'S POLLEN COUNT
SAM GEIGER
& COUNTERS INC.
TODAY'S POLLEN COUNT
SAM GEIGER
& COUNTERS INC.
PING
TODAY'S POLLEN COUNT

hospital . . .

SAM GEIGER & COUNTERS INC.
BLOOD PRESSURE THIS WEEK
TODAYS POLLEN COUNT
MONACO STOCK UP 30%..
Hey! Where *you* going, Smilby?
. . . the boss said I could knock off early. I have to have an operation.
... COME TO THE AID OF THEIR PARTY ...
. . . that Smilby! . . . always finding some way to get out of work!
DING!

Next, in 'Medical, here's the dramatic way going to the

Lance! You played beautifully tonight! Go out and take a curtain call!
Stop this farce, Amanda! I played terribly and you know it! .... this horrible pain I get when I laugh. This pain in my neck! I'll never play the violin again!
The violin you played terrible, but the scrabble game before that, you played beautifully tonight!
Lance! I've brought a doctor to look at you despite the fact that you have been putting off seeing a doctor because you are afraid of what you might find out because you are afraid to face the truth.
TAP TAP
And mainly because I first want to join a Blue Cross plan which will make it cheaper.
I'm Konrad Strainer, Doctor of Medicine. Case in point.. Lance Follicle. Say 'Ahh'

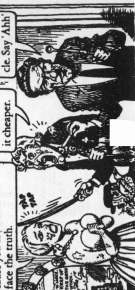

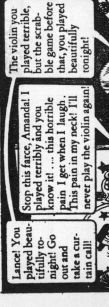

hospital is . . .

Here! you may keep the stick!
Mr. Follicle . . . my examination reveals the existence of inspissated mucus on the masses of lymphoid tissues between the anterior and posterior pillars of the fauces indicating a suppurative condition further characterized by hyperaemia and exudation. Enucleation is necessary.
You *mean* . . . ?
Yes . . .
Y-you're *positive?* T-there *can't be a mistake?*
No.
we gotta take out tonsils.
(background music strikes heavy, ominous chords here)

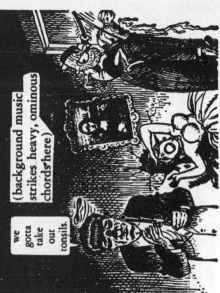

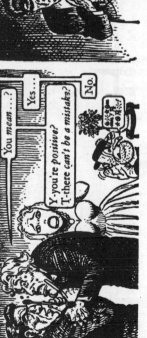

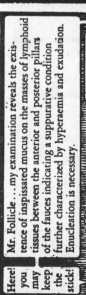

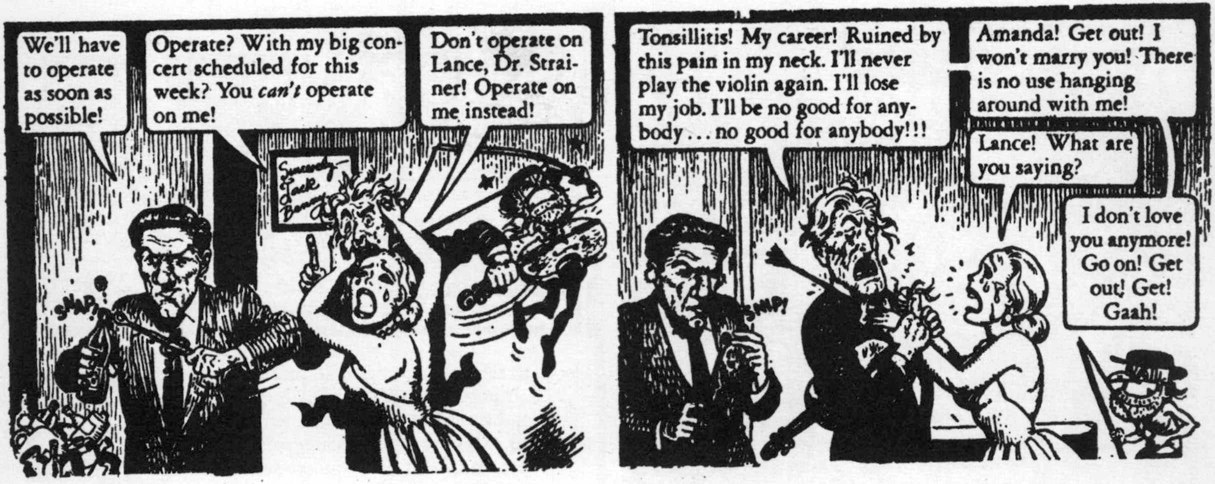
We'll have to operate as soon as possible!
SNAP!
Operate? With my big concert scheduled for this week? You *can't* operate on me!
Don't operate on Lance, Dr. Strainer! Operate on me instead!
Tonsillitis! My career! Ruined by this pain in my neck. I'll never play the violin again. I'll lose my job. I'll be no good for anybody . . . no good for anybody!!!
SNIP!
Amanda! Get out! I won't marry you! There is no use hanging around with me!
Lance! What are you saying?
I don't love you anymore! Go on! Get out! Get! Gaah!

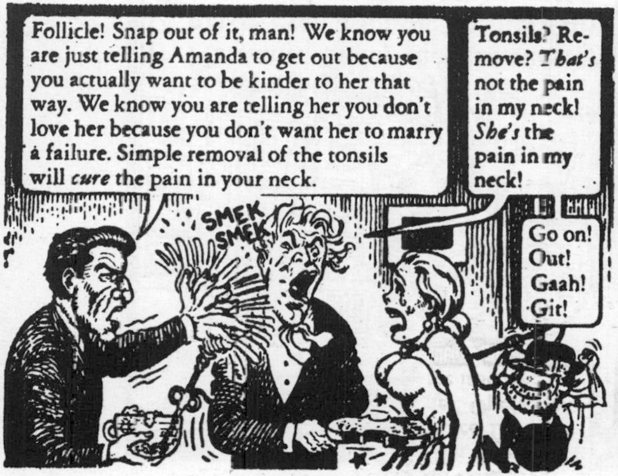
Follicle! Snap out of it, man! We know you are just telling Amanda to get out because you actually want to be kinder to her that way. We know you are telling her you don't love her because you don't want her to marry a failure. Simple removal of the tonsils will *cure* the pain in your neck.
SMEK SMEK
Tonsils? Remove? *That's* not the pain in my neck! *She's* the pain in my neck!
Go on! Out! Gaah! Git!

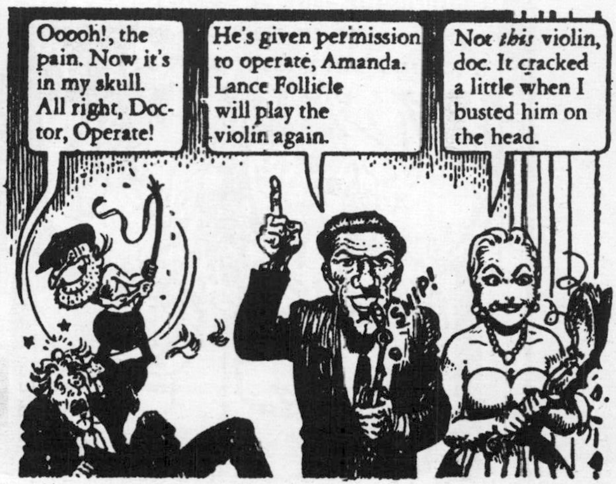
Ooooh!, the pain. Now it's in my skull. All right, Doctor, Operate!
He's given permission to operate, Amanda. Lance Follicle will play the violin again.
SNIP!
Not *this* violin, doc. It cracked a little when I busted him on the head.

Operation Scene is most (ugh) fascinating of all.

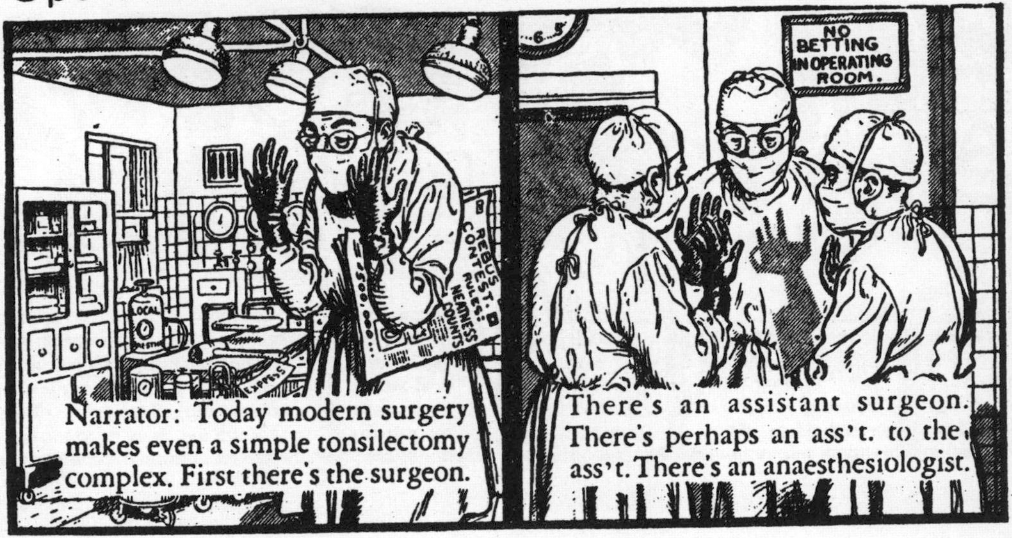
REBUS CONTEST. RULES: NEATNESS COUNTS
$500,000...
LOCAL
EXPRESS
Narrator: Today modern surgery makes even a simple tonsilectomy complex. First there's the surgeon.
NO BETTING IN OPERATING ROOM.
There's an assistant surgeon. There's perhaps an ass't. to the ass't. There's an anaesthesiologist.

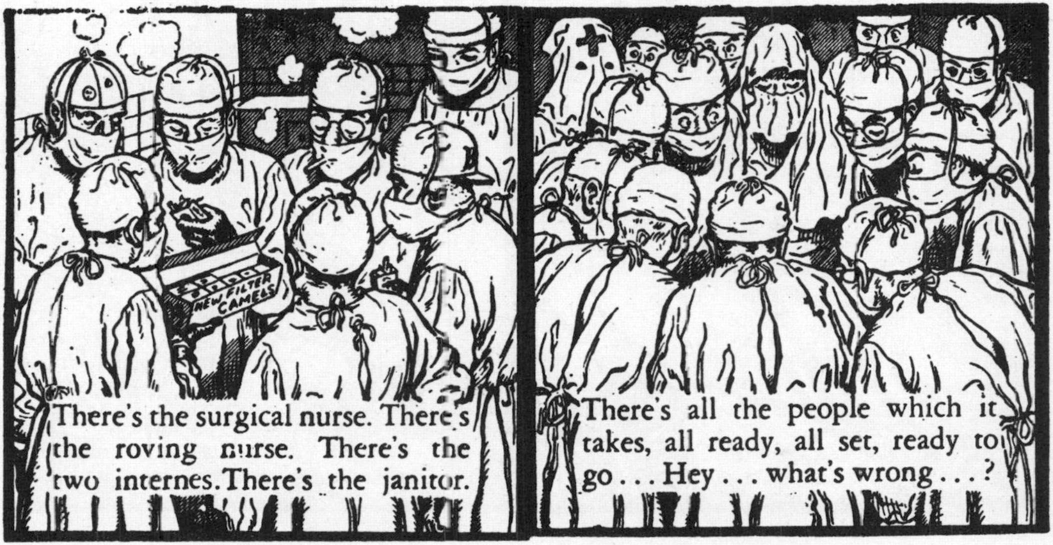
NEW FILTER CAMELS
There's the surgical nurse. There's the roving nurse. There's the two internes. There's the janitor.
There's all the people which it takes, all ready, all set, ready to go . . . Hey . . . what's wrong . . . ?

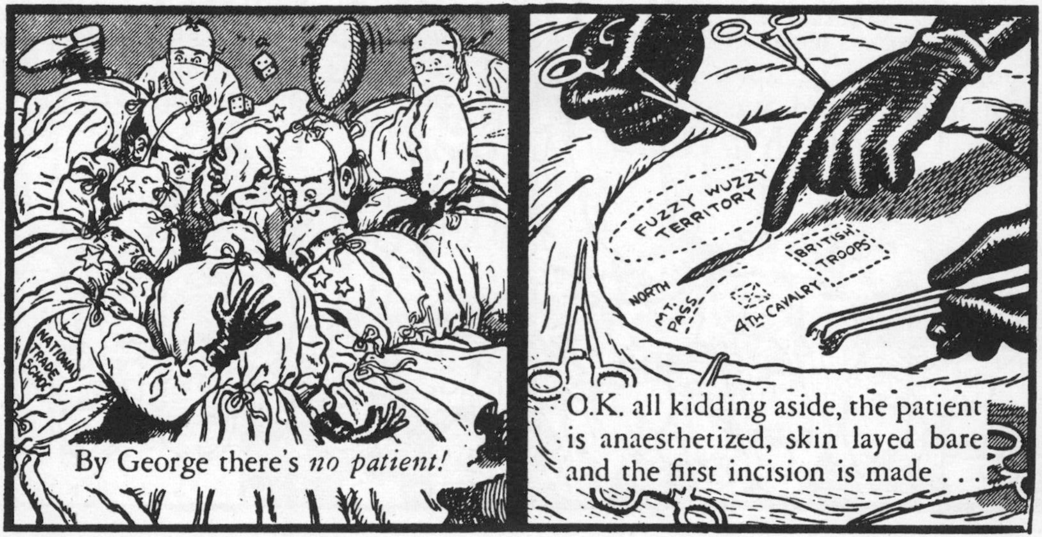
NATIONAL TRADE SCHOOL
By George there's *no patient!*
FUZZY WUZZY TERRITORY
BRITISH TROOPS
NORTH
MT. PASS
4TH CAVALRY
O.K. all kidding aside, the patient is anaesthetized, skin layed bare and the first incision is made . . .

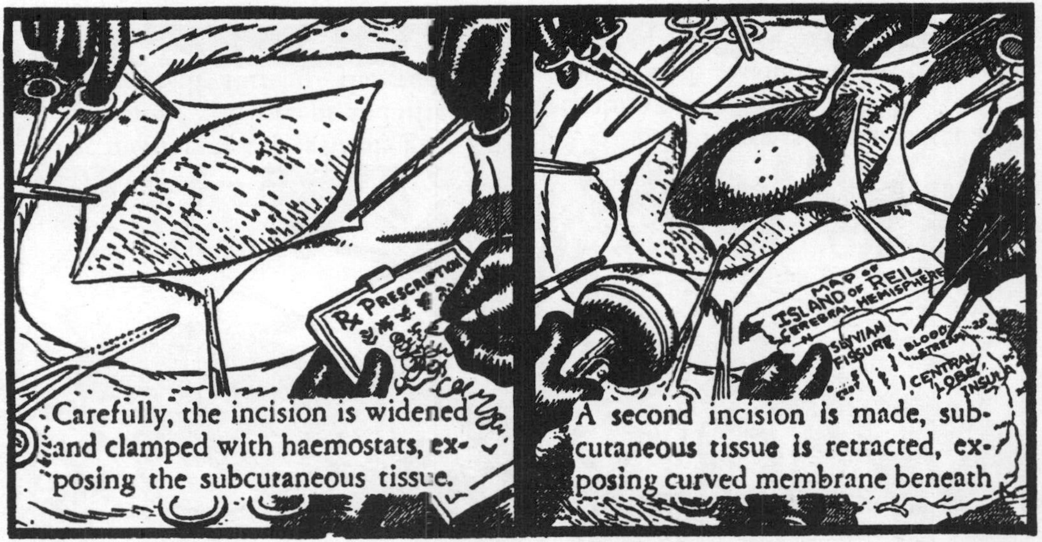
Carefully, the incision is widened and clamped with haemostats, exposing the subcutaneous tissue.
Rx PRESCRIPTION
MAP OF ISLAND OF REIL
CEREBRAL HEMISPHERE
SYLVIAN FISSURE
BLOOD STREAM
CENTRAL LOBE
INSULA
A second incision is made, subcutaneous tissue is retracted, exposing curved membrane beneath

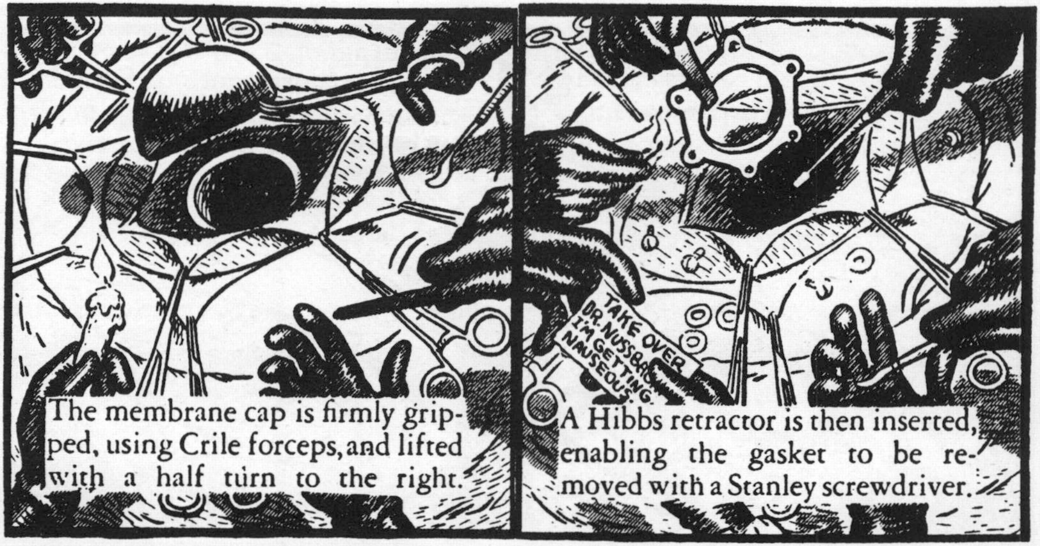
The membrane cap is firmly gripped, using Crile forceps, and lifted with a half turn to the right.
TAKE OVER DR. NUSSBA I'M GETTING NAUSEOUS.
A Hibbs retractor is then inserted, enabling the gasket to be removed with a Stanley screwdriver.

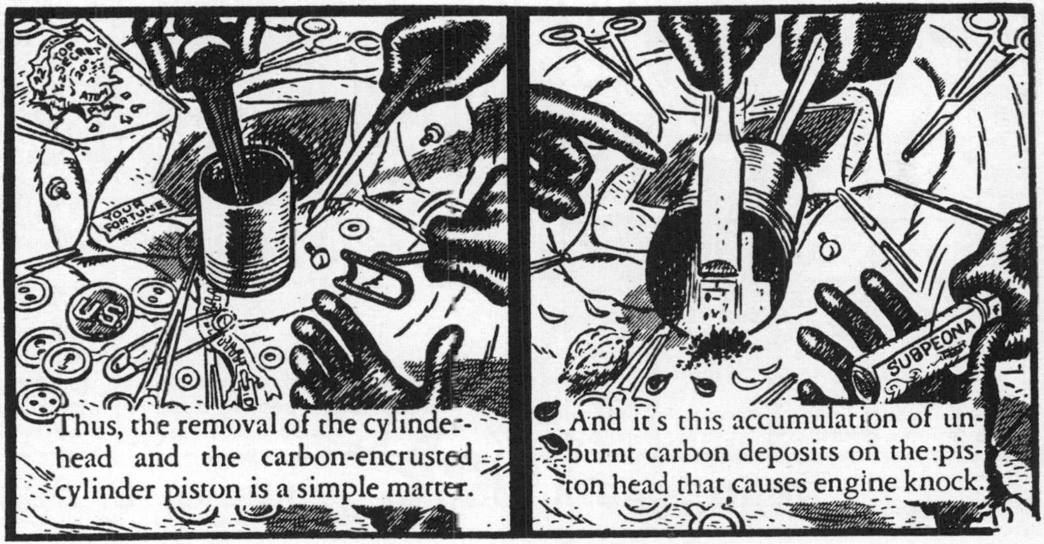
YOUR FORTUNE
US
Thus, the removal of the cylinder-head and the carbon-encrusted cylinder piston is a simple matter.
SUBPEONA
And it's this accumulation of unburnt carbon deposits on the piston head that causes engine knock.

Ending in "Medical" is happy ever after.

Well, Lance . . . it's one month since we took out your tonsils so today is the day.
Yes . . . that uneasy day when you remove the bandages, when I will know if the operation is a success, when I will know if I'll play the violin again, when I will know what the hospital bill comes to.
Dr. Strainer is removing the bandages!
The background music is reaching a wild crescendo!
Will the operation be a success?
Will Lance Follicle play the violin again?
Will Success Spoil Rock Hunter?
fade out here

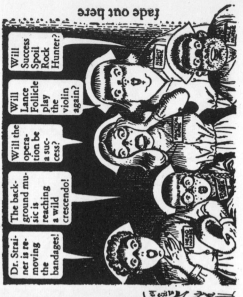

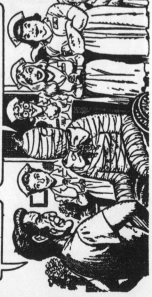

fade back one week later

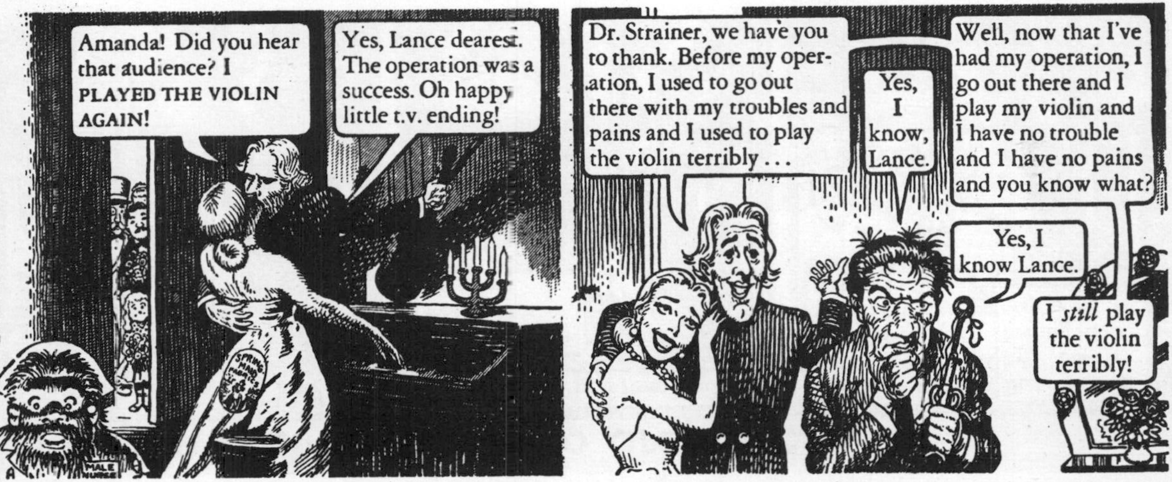

Amanda! Did you hear that audience? I PLAYED THE VIOLIN AGAIN!
Yes, Lance dearest. The operation was a success. Oh happy little t.v. ending!
MALE NURSE
Dr. Strainer, we have you to thank. Before my operation, I used to go out there with my troubles and pains and I used to play the violin terribly . . .
Yes, I know, Lance.
Well, now that I've had my operation, I go out there and I play my violin and I have no trouble and I have no pains and you know what?
Yes, I know Lance.
I *still* play the violin terribly!

Ending in real-life is not so dramatic.

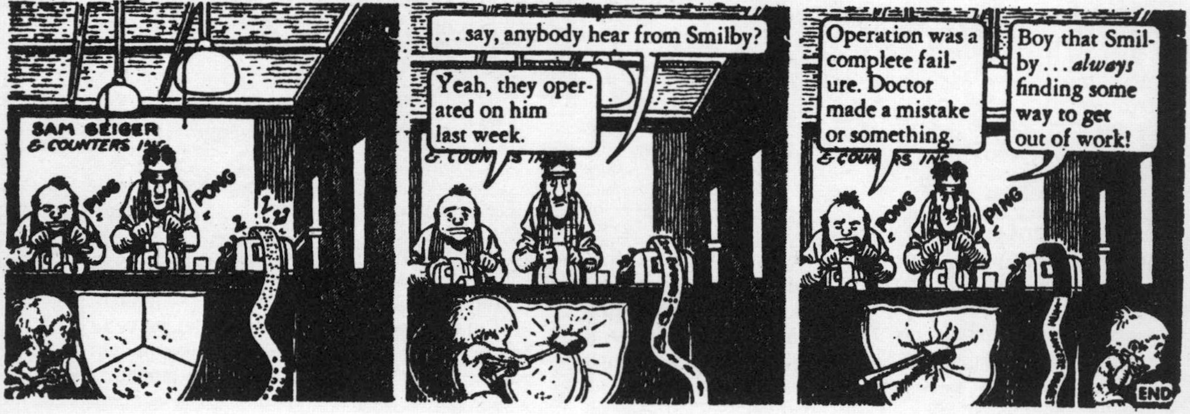
SAM SEIGER
& COUNTERS INC.
PING
PONG
... say, anybody hear from Smilby?
Yeah, they operated on him last week.
Operation was a complete failure. Doctor made a mistake or something.
PONG
PING
Boy that Smilby ... *always* finding some way to get out of work!
END

Report from Abroad—I: We are proud to announce that the purpose of THE BEDSIDE MAD is to inform as well as to entertain. Serious readers are interested in things like current events. We must therefore turn serious for a moment to bring you this report from a famous analyst on Egypt. Yes, it is well to watch Egypt, keystone of the East. In Egypt the decisions of tomorrow will be made in the future. We are sure that this article will stress that fact even more so, and so we present this article called . . .

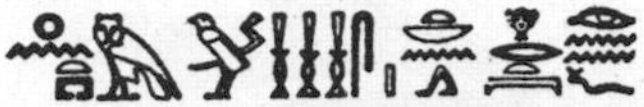

by...

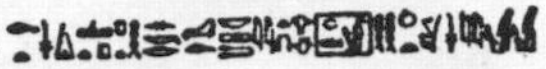

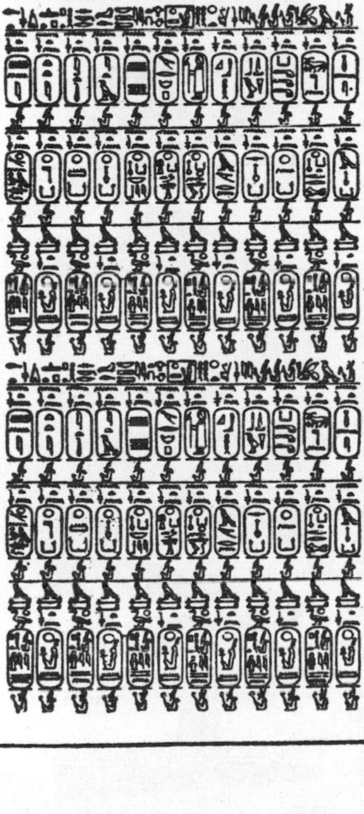

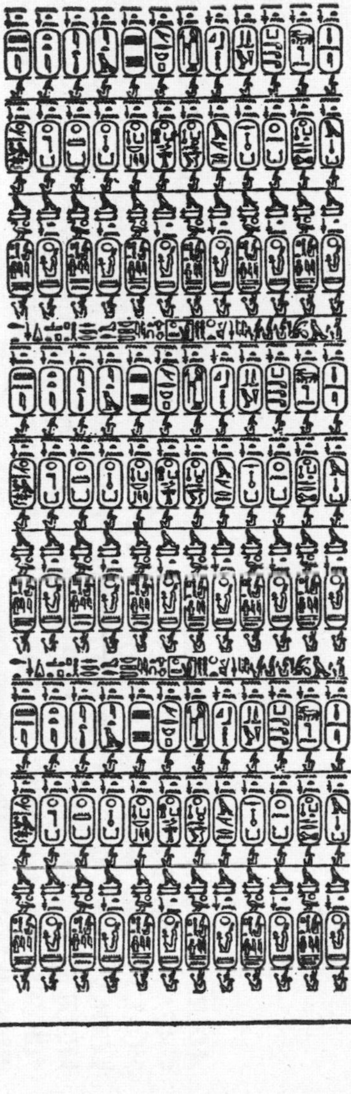

ADULT WESTERN DEPT: HERB IS AN ALL-TIME, NEVER-TO-BE-FORGOTTEN, GREAT CLASSIC THAT CHANGED THE COURSE OF WESTERN HISTORY . . . HOLLYWOOD WESTERN HISTORY, THAT IS . . . SCENE: A HOT SUMMER SUN LOOKS DOWN ON A TERRIFIED COW-TOWN WHERE WORD IS FLYING FROM MOUTH TO MOUTH . . . "GOSH! KILLER DILLER MILLER IS OUT OF JAIL!" . . . "CHEE! HE'S A-COMIN' TO TOWN!" "DURN! HE'S A-COMIN' ON THE TRAIN?" . . . "HOOH! WHEN'S HE A-COMIN'?" . . .

'HAH! NOON!'

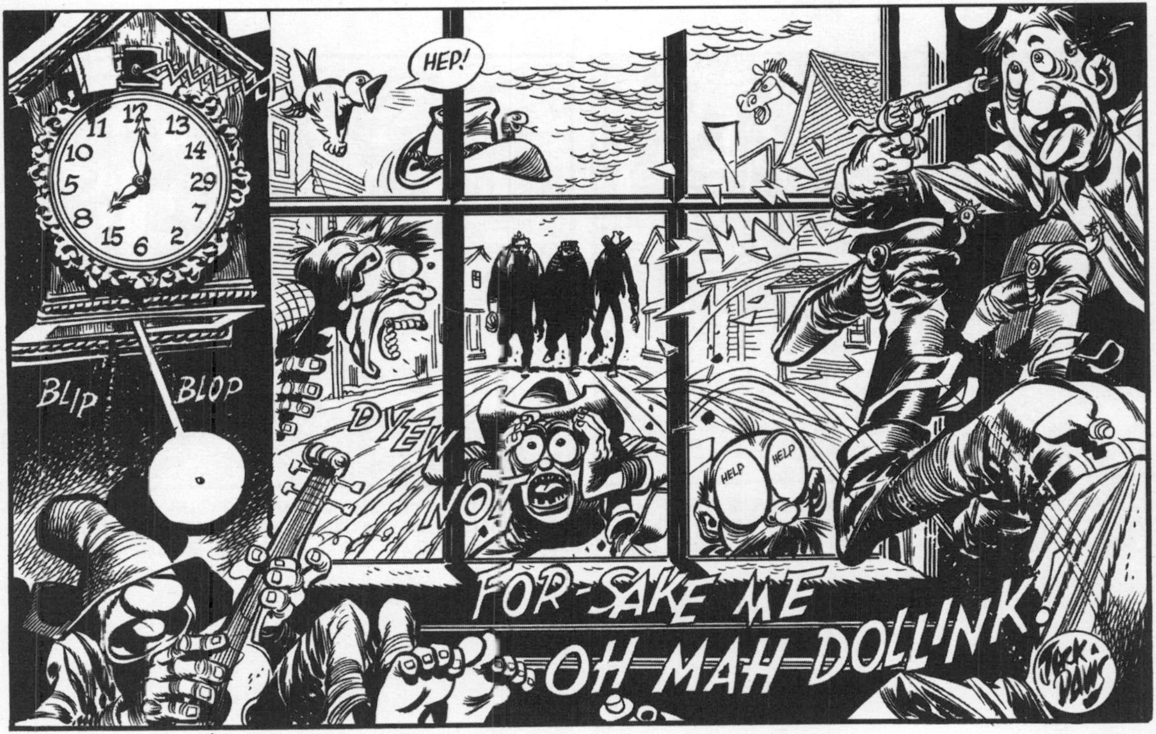
HEP!
BLIP
BLOP
DYEW
NOT
HELP
HELP
FOR-SAKE ME
OH MAH DOLLINK!
Jack Davis

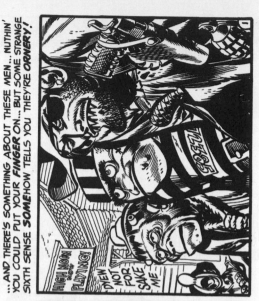

THREE MEN STRIDE DOWN THE DUSTY STREET WHICH IS QUIET BUT FOR THE QUICK SCUTTLING OF CITIZENS DISAPPEARING INTO DOORWAYS AND RAIN BARRELS!
ON THIS OW WEDDIN DEY...
...AND THERE'S SOMETHING ABOUT THESE MEN... NUTHIN' YOU COULD PUT YOUR **FINGER** ON... BUT SOME STRANGE SIXTH SENSE **SOME**HOW TELLS YOU THEY'RE ***ORNERY!***
HIGH NOON NOW PLAYING!
DYEW NOT FOR SAKE ME

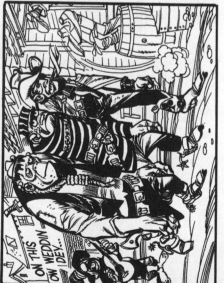

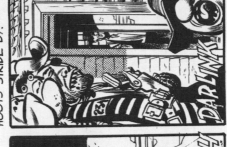

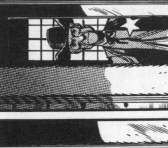

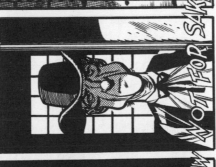

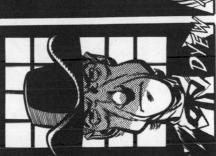

...OFF TO THE SIDE, ONLY **ONE** MAN IS BRAVE ENOUGH TO STAND HIS GROUND!
...ONLY **ONE** MAN DOES NOT MOVE AN INCH FROM WHERE HE STANDS!
...ONLY **ONE** MAN TAKES NO STEP BACKWARD AS HE SURVEYS THE SCENE!
...MARSHALL KANE CALMLY WATCHES THE THREE OWL-HOOTS STRIDE BY!
DYEW NOT FORSAKE ME OH MAH DARLINK
23

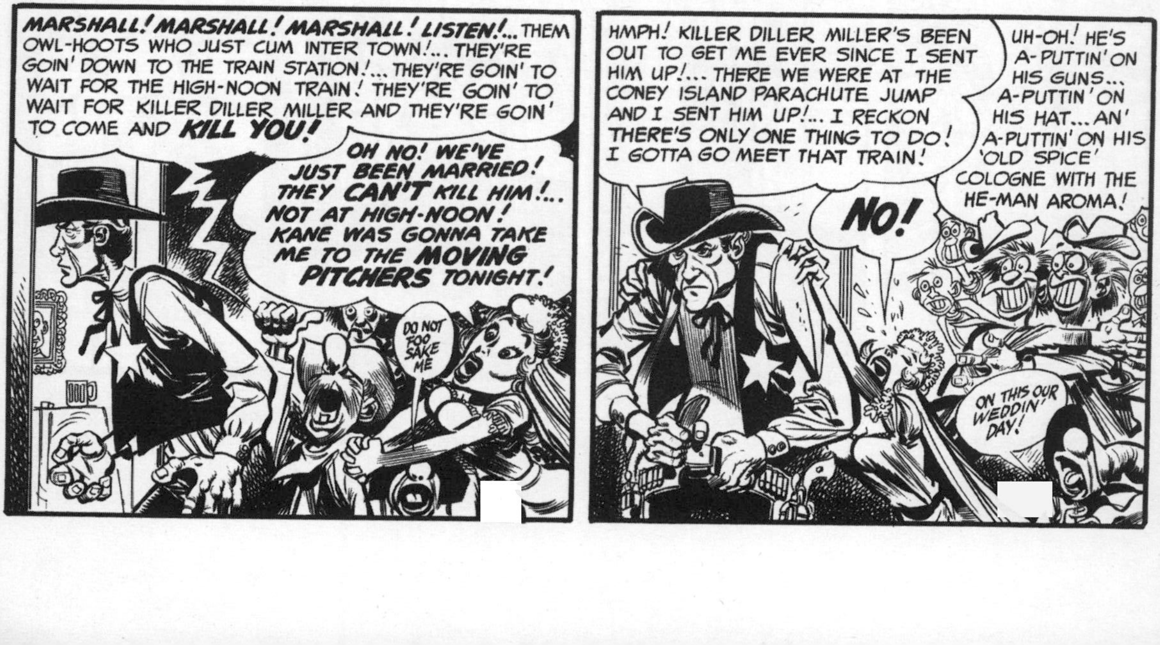
MARSHALL! MARSHALL! MARSHALL! LISTEN!... THEM OWL-HOOTS WHO JUST CUM INTER TOWN!... THEY'RE GOIN' DOWN TO THE TRAIN STATION!... THEY'RE GOIN' TO WAIT FOR THE HIGH-NOON TRAIN! THEY'RE GOIN' TO WAIT FOR KILLER DILLER MILLER AND THEY'RE GOIN' TO COME AND KILL YOU!
OH NO! WE'VE JUST BEEN MARRIED! THEY CAN'T KILL HIM!... NOT AT HIGH-NOON! KANE WAS GONNA TAKE ME TO THE MOVING PITCHERS TONIGHT!
DO NOT FOO SAKE ME
HMPH! KILLER DILLER MILLER'S BEEN OUT TO GET ME EVER SINCE I SENT HIM UP!... THERE WE WERE AT THE CONEY ISLAND PARACHUTE JUMP AND I SENT HIM UP!... I RECKON THERE'S ONLY ONE THING TO DO! I GOTTA GO MEET THAT TRAIN!
UH-OH! HE'S A-PUTTIN' ON HIS GUNS... A-PUTTIN' ON HIS HAT... AN' A-PUTTIN' ON HIS 'OLD SPICE' COLOGNE WITH THE HE-MAN AROMA!
NO!
ON THIS OUR WEDDIN' DAY!

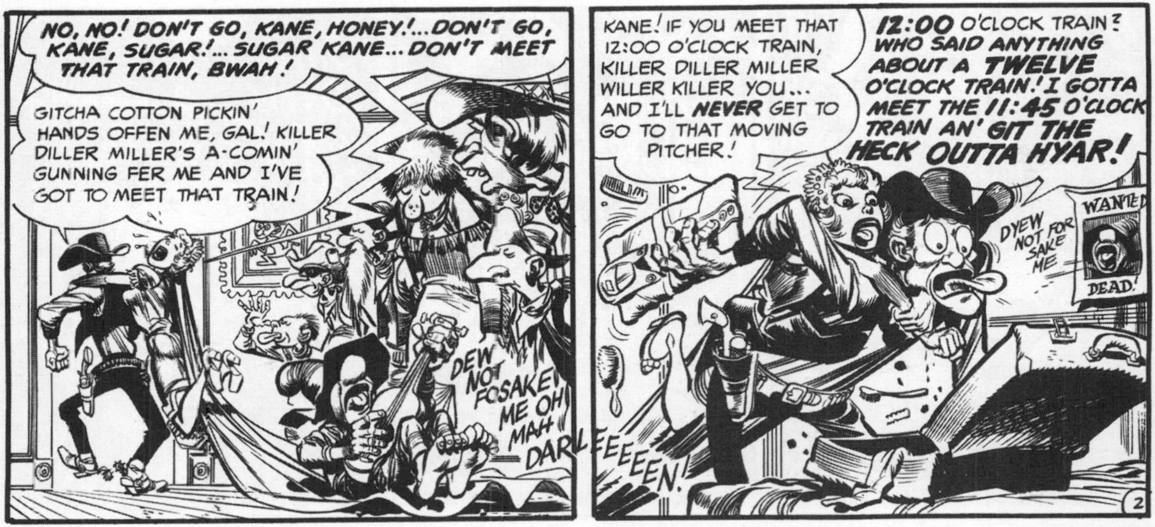

NO, NO! DON'T GO, KANE, HONEY!... DON'T GO, KANE, SUGAR!... SUGAR KANE... DON'T MEET THAT TRAIN, BWAH!
GITCHA COTTON PICKIN' HANDS OFFEN ME, GAL! KILLER DILLER MILLER'S A-COMIN' GUNNING FER ME AND I'VE GOT TO MEET THAT TRAIN!
DEW NOT FOSAKE ME OH MAH DARLEEEEEN!
KANE! IF YOU MEET THAT 12:00 O'CLOCK TRAIN, KILLER DILLER MILLER WILLER KILLER YOU... AND I'LL NEVER GET TO GO TO THAT MOVING PITCHER!
12:00 O'CLOCK TRAIN? WHO SAID ANYTHING ABOUT A TWELVE O'CLOCK TRAIN! I GOTTA MEET THE 11:45 O'CLOCK TRAIN AN' GIT THE HECK OUTTA HYAR!
DYEW NOT FOR SAKE ME
WANTED
DEAD!
2

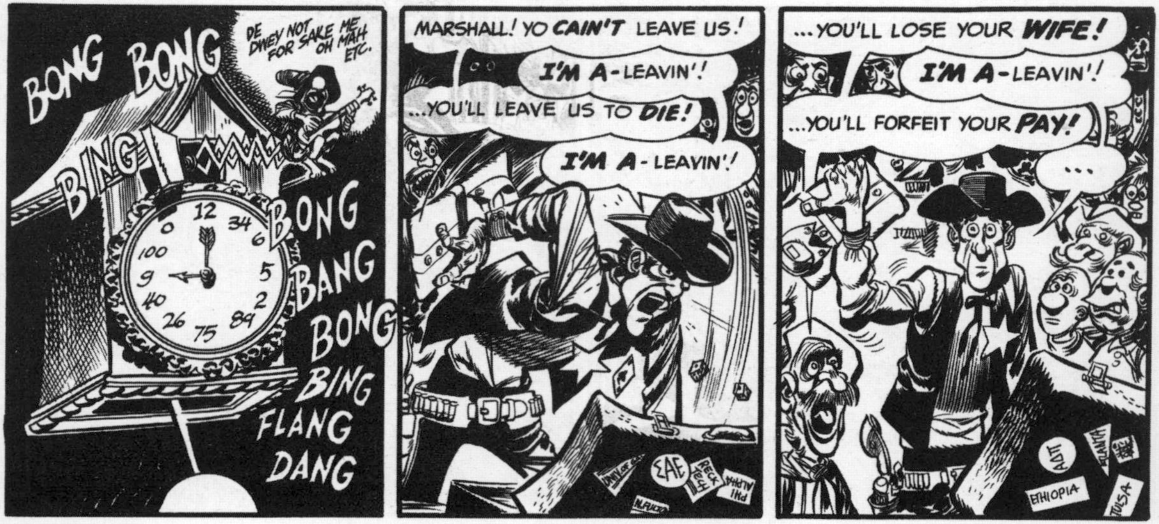
BONG BONG
DE DWEY NOT FOR SAKE ME OH MAH ETC.
BING
BONG
BANG
BONG
BING
FLANG
DANG
MARSHALL! YO CAIN'T LEAVE US!
I'M A-LEAVIN'!
...YOU'LL LEAVE US TO DIE!
I'M A-LEAVIN'!
ΣΑΕ
RECK TECH
PHI ALPHA
...YOU'LL LOSE YOUR WIFE!
I'M A-LEAVIN'!
...YOU'LL FORFEIT YOUR PAY!
...
ETHIOPIA
TULSA

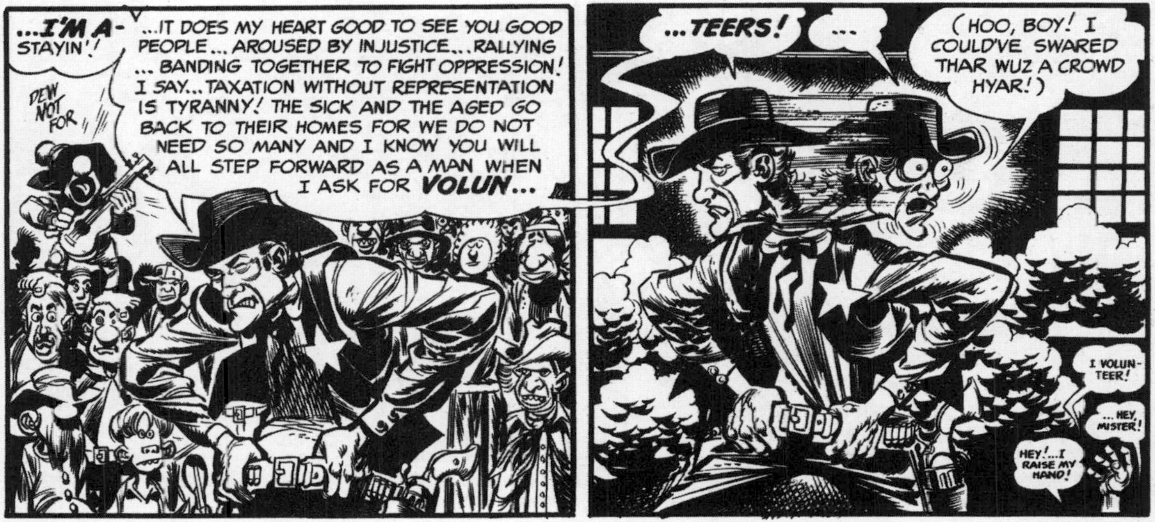

...I'M A-STAYIN'!
DEW NOT FOR
...IT DOES MY HEART GOOD TO SEE YOU GOOD PEOPLE... AROUSED BY INJUSTICE... RALLYING ... BANDING TOGETHER TO FIGHT OPPRESSION! I SAY... TAXATION WITHOUT REPRESENTATION IS TYRANNY! THE SICK AND THE AGED GO BACK TO THEIR HOMES FOR WE DO NOT NEED SO MANY AND I KNOW YOU WILL ALL STEP FORWARD AS A MAN WHEN I ASK FOR **VOLUN...**
...TEERS!
...
(HOO, BOY! I COULD'VE SWARED THAR WUZ A CROWD HYAR!)
I VOLUN-TEER!
...HEY, MISTER!
HEY!...I RAISE MY HAND!

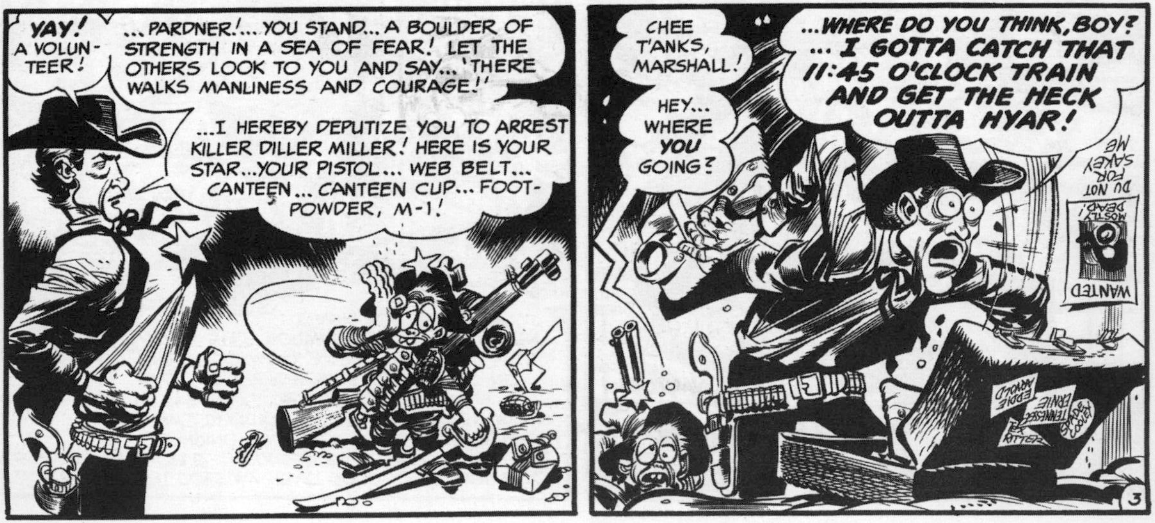
YAY! A VOLUNTEER!
...PARDNER!... YOU STAND... A BOULDER OF STRENGTH IN A SEA OF FEAR! LET THE OTHERS LOOK TO YOU AND SAY... 'THERE WALKS MANLINESS AND COURAGE!'
...I HEREBY DEPUTIZE YOU TO ARREST KILLER DILLER MILLER! HERE IS YOUR STAR...YOUR PISTOL... WEB BELT... CANTEEN... CANTEEN CUP... FOOT-POWDER, M-1!
CHEE T'ANKS, MARSHALL!
HEY... WHERE YOU GOING?
...WHERE DO YOU THINK, BOY? ... I GOTTA CATCH THAT 11:45 O'CLOCK TRAIN AND GET THE HECK OUTTA HYAR!
WANTED
MOSTLY DEAD!
DU NOT FOR SAKEY ME
EDDIE ARNOLD
TENNESSEE ERNIE
TEX RITTER
SPADE COOLEY
3

BONG
BUNG
BANG
NEVER MORE
BINGO
BONG
BANG
BLANG
BONK
BONG
BOP
DYEW NOT FOR SAK...
MARSHALL! YO CAIN'T LEAVE US!
I'M A- LEAVIN'!
...THEY'LL BURN THE TOWN!
I'M A- LEAVIN'!
...THEY'LL GUN YORE GRANMAW!
I'M A-LEAVIN'!
...WHO'LL WATCH THE STORE?
...I'M A-LEAVIN'!

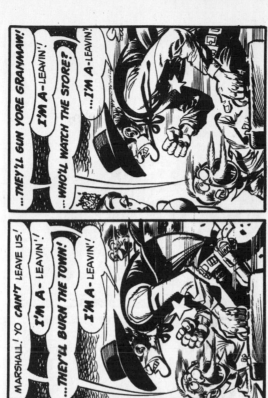

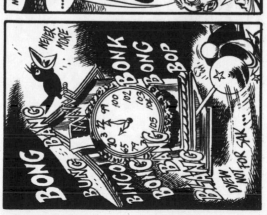

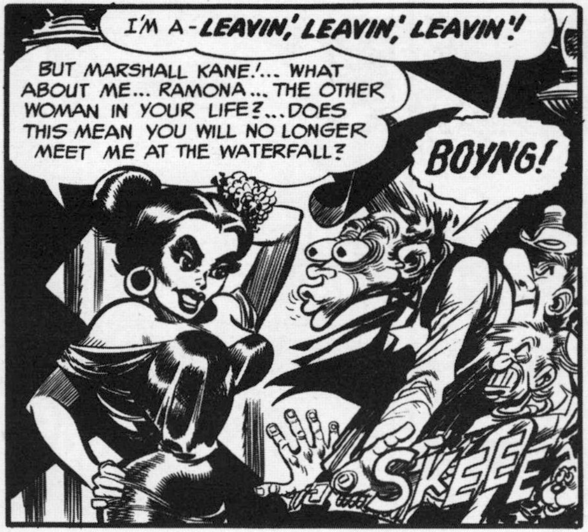
I'M A-LEAVIN,' LEAVIN,' LEAVIN'!
BUT MARSHALL KANE!... WHAT ABOUT ME... RAMONA... THE OTHER WOMAN IN YOUR LIFE?...DOES THIS MEAN YOU WILL NO LONGER MEET ME AT THE WATERFALL?
BOYNG!
SKEEEE

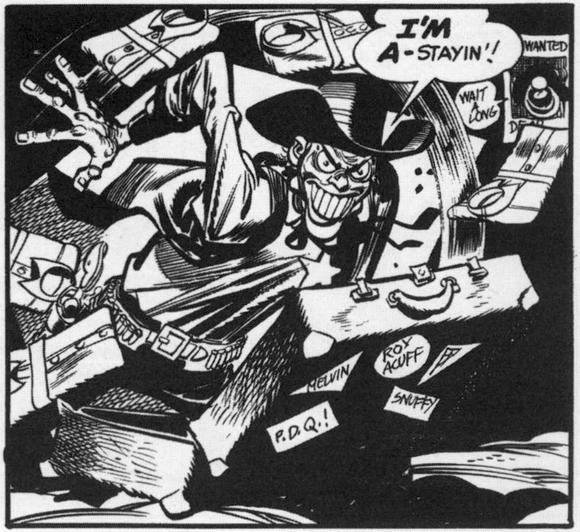
I'M A-STAYIN'!
WANTED
WAIT A LONG
MELVIN
ROY ACUFF
SNUFFY
P.D.Q.!

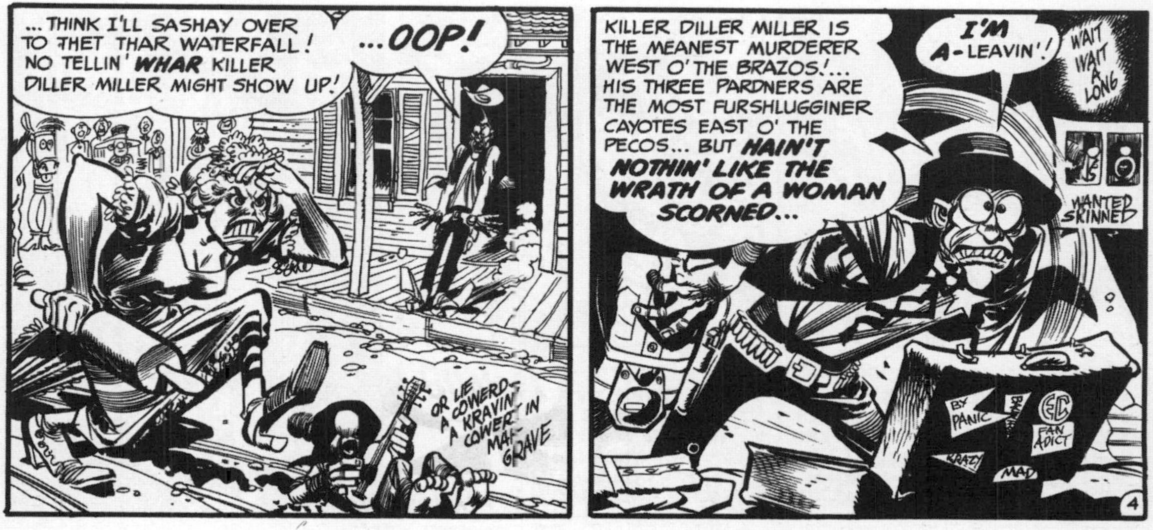

...THINK I'LL SASHAY OVER TO THET THAR WATERFALL! NO TELLIN' **WHAR** KILLER DILLER MILLER MIGHT SHOW UP!
...OOP!
OR LIE A COWERD- A KRAVIN' COWERT IN MAH GRAVE
KILLER DILLER MILLER IS THE MEANEST MURDERER WEST O' THE BRAZOS!... HIS THREE PARDNERS ARE THE MOST FURSHLUGGINER CAYOTES EAST O' THE PECOS... BUT **HAIN'T NOTHIN' LIKE THE WRATH OF A WOMAN SCORNED...**
I'M A-LEAVIN'!
WAIT WAIT A LONG
WANTED SKINNED
BY PANIC
KRAZY
MAD
EC
FAN ADICT
4

BAM! BAM!
OPEN UP!
I'M LOCKED IN!
11 12 33 78 29 45 1,000 13 59 92 SHIFT 45
BONG BONG ETC.
KANE!
...YOU'VE COME BACK! ...WELL...IT'S TOO LATE! YOU LEFT YOUR JOB AND I NOW HAVE IT AND I'M THE NEW TOWN MARSHALL!... THAT'S MY NAME... MARSHALL FLOODNICK!
FLOODNICK, YOU NO-GOODNICK... I KNOW YOU'RE IN CA-HOOTS WITH THE OWL-HOOTS AND DON'T GIVE TWO-HOOTS FOR THIS TOWN-HOOTS! NOW LEMME INTO THE MARSHALL'S OFFICE OR I'LL GIVE YOU SUCH A **HIT**...
ZZ ZZ Z
HE MADE A VOW WHILE IN STATE PEN

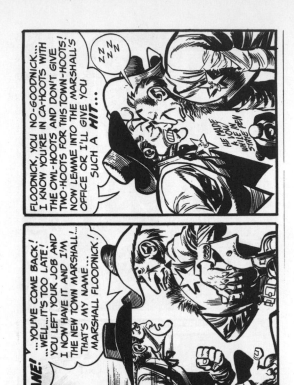

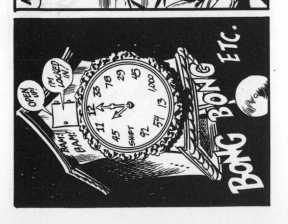

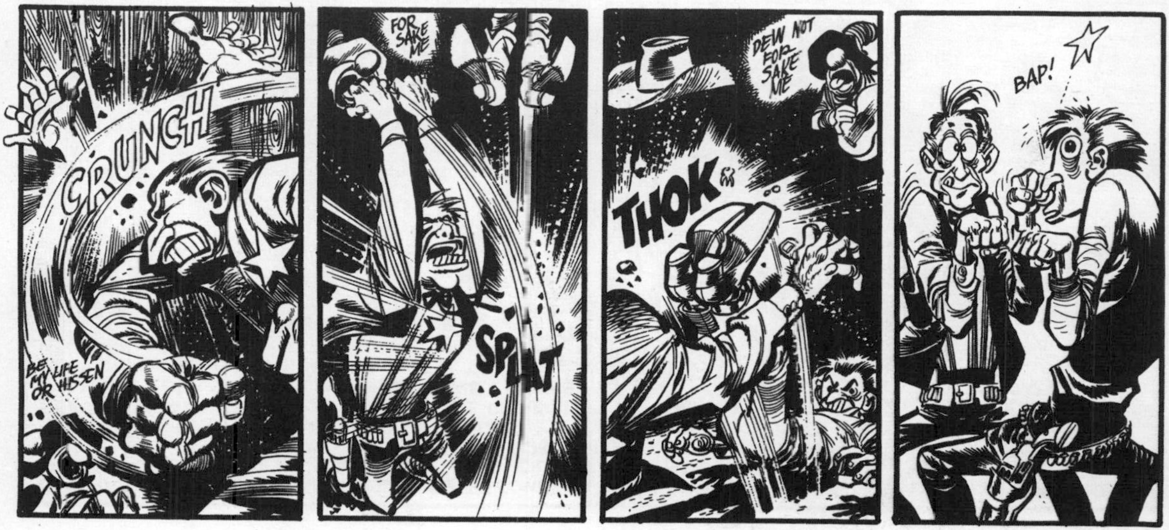
CRUNCH
BE MY LIFE OR HISSEN
FOR SAKE ME
SPLAT
DEW NOT FOR SAKE ME
THOK
BAP!

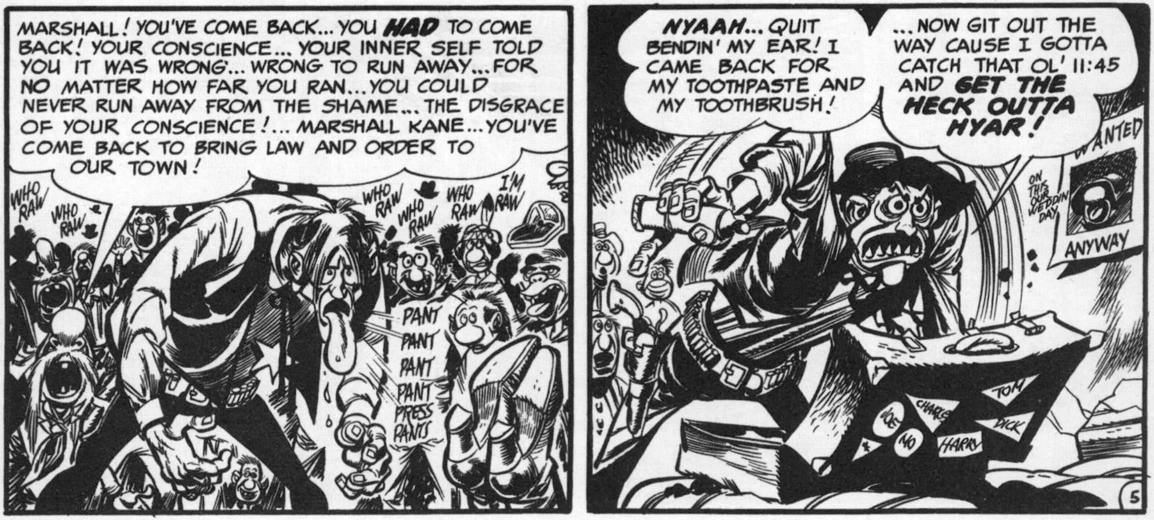
MARSHALL! YOU'VE COME BACK... YOU **HAD** TO COME BACK! YOUR CONSCIENCE... YOUR INNER SELF TOLD YOU IT WAS WRONG... WRONG TO RUN AWAY... FOR NO MATTER HOW FAR YOU RAN... YOU COULD NEVER RUN AWAY FROM THE SHAME... THE DISGRACE OF YOUR CONSCIENCE!... MARSHALL KANE... YOU'VE COME BACK TO BRING LAW AND ORDER TO OUR TOWN!
WHO RAW
WHO RAW
WHO RAW
WHO RAW
WHO RAW
I'M RAW
PANT PANT PANT PANT PRESS PANTS
NYAAH... QUIT BENDIN' MY EAR! I CAME BACK FOR MY TOOTHPASTE AND MY TOOTHBRUSH!
...NOW GIT OUT THE WAY CAUSE I GOTTA CATCH THAT OL' 11:45 AND **GET THE HECK OUTTA HYAR!**
WANTED
ON THIS OUR WEDDIN DAY
ANYWAY
TOM
CHARLE
DICK
JOE
NO
HARRY
5

HIGH NOON
BONG 12 TIMES
TWOOOOOOOIE
OH TO BE TORN TWIX LUV AND DUTY
HOWDY, 'KILLER'!
THAT'S A GOOD DISGUISE, 'KILLER'!
BUT...
BUT... BUT...
BUT, BUT BUT...
HYAR'S YOUR GUNS, 'KILLER'!

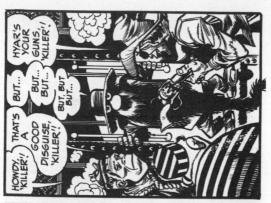

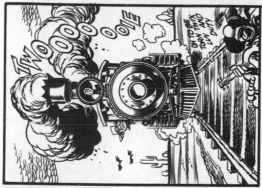

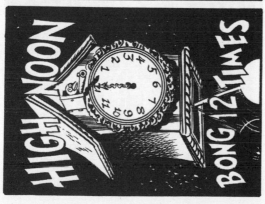

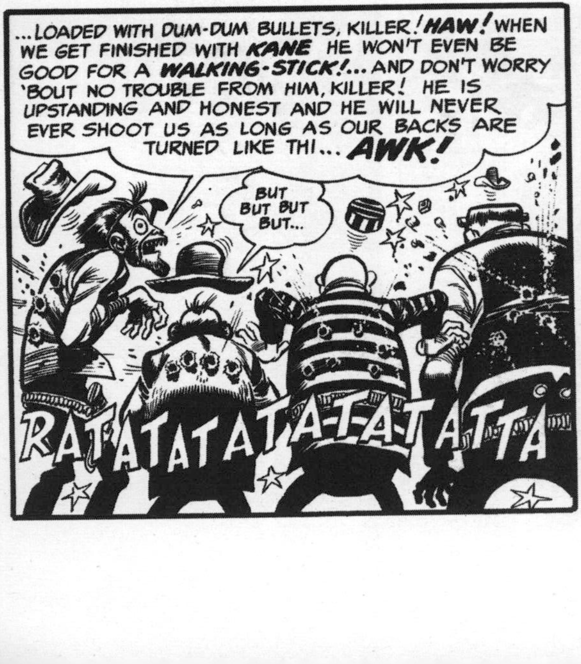
...LOADED WITH DUM-DUM BULLETS, KILLER! **HAW!** WHEN WE GET FINISHED WITH **KANE** HE WON'T EVEN BE GOOD FOR A **WALKING-STICK!**... AND DON'T WORRY 'BOUT NO TROUBLE FROM HIM, KILLER! HE IS UPSTANDING AND HONEST AND HE WILL NEVER EVER SHOOT US AS LONG AS OUR BACKS ARE TURNED LIKE THI... **AWK!**
BUT BUT BUT BUT...
RATATATATATATATATTA

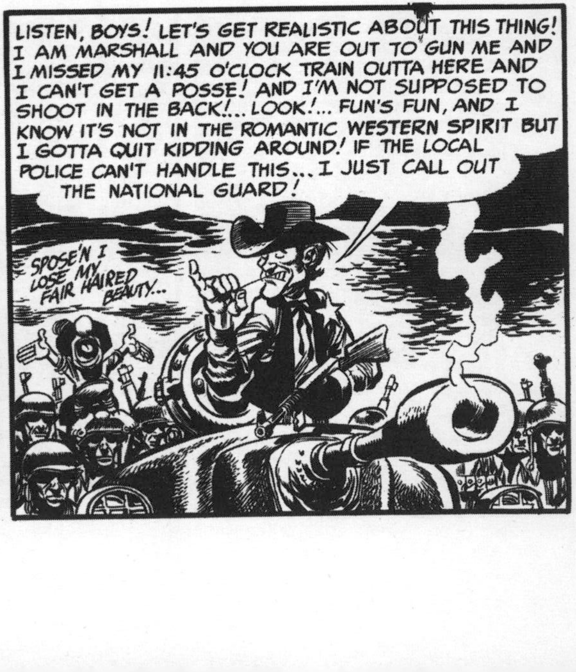
LISTEN, BOYS! LET'S GET REALISTIC ABOUT THIS THING! I AM MARSHALL AND YOU ARE OUT TO GUN ME AND I MISSED MY 11:45 O'CLOCK TRAIN OUTTA HERE AND I CAN'T GET A POSSE! AND I'M NOT SUPPOSED TO SHOOT IN THE BACK!... LOOK!... FUN'S FUN, AND I KNOW IT'S NOT IN THE ROMANTIC WESTERN SPIRIT BUT I GOTTA QUIT KIDDING AROUND! IF THE LOCAL POLICE CAN'T HANDLE THIS... I JUST CALL OUT THE NATIONAL GUARD!
SPOSE'N I LOSE MY FAIR HAIRED BEAUTY...

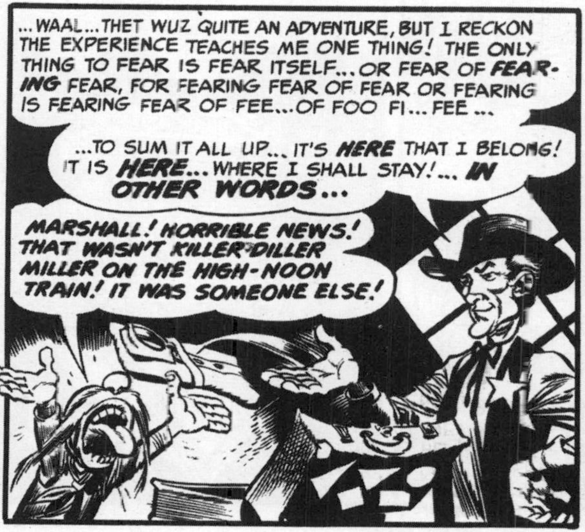
...WAAL...THET WUZ QUITE AN ADVENTURE, BUT I RECKON THE EXPERIENCE TEACHES ME ONE THING! THE ONLY THING TO FEAR IS FEAR ITSELF...OR FEAR OF FEARING FEAR, FOR FEARING FEAR OF FEAR OR FEARING IS FEARING FEAR OF FEE...OF FOO FI...FEE...
...TO SUM IT ALL UP... IT'S HERE THAT I BELONG! IT IS HERE... WHERE I SHALL STAY!... IN OTHER WORDS...
MARSHALL! HORRIBLE NEWS! THAT WASN'T KILLER DILLER MILLER ON THE HIGH-NOON TRAIN! IT WAS SOMEONE ELSE!

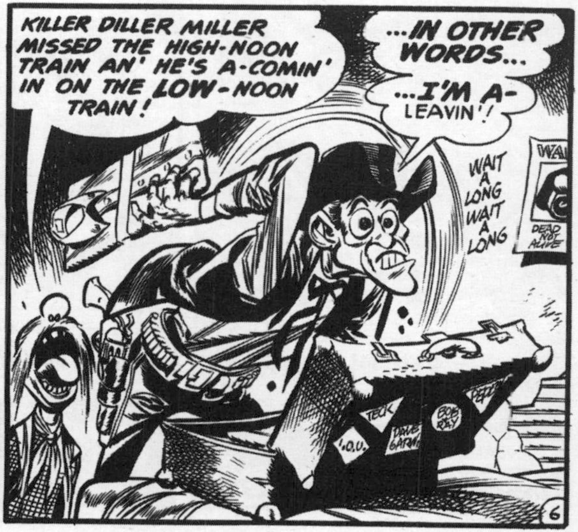
KILLER DILLER MILLER MISSED THE HIGH-NOON TRAIN AN' HE'S A-COMIN' IN ON THE LOW-NOON TRAIN!
...IN OTHER WORDS...
...I'M A-LEAVIN'!
WAIT A LONG WAIT A LONG
DEAD NOT ALIVE
TECK
BOB RAY
DAVE GARM
I.O.U.
6

DING!
OUT TO LUNCH
HERE WE GO AGAIN!
I'M A- LEAVIN'!
...HE'LL KILL US!
I'M A- LEAVIN'!
...HE'LL BLOW OUR BRAINS OUT!
I'M A- LEAVIN'!
I'LL BLOW YER HEAD OFF!
I'M A- STAYIN'!

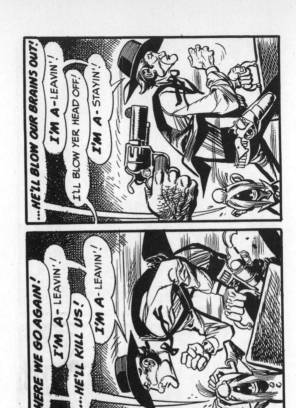

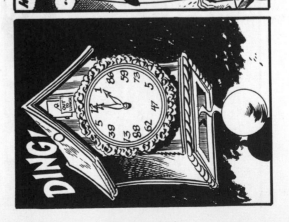

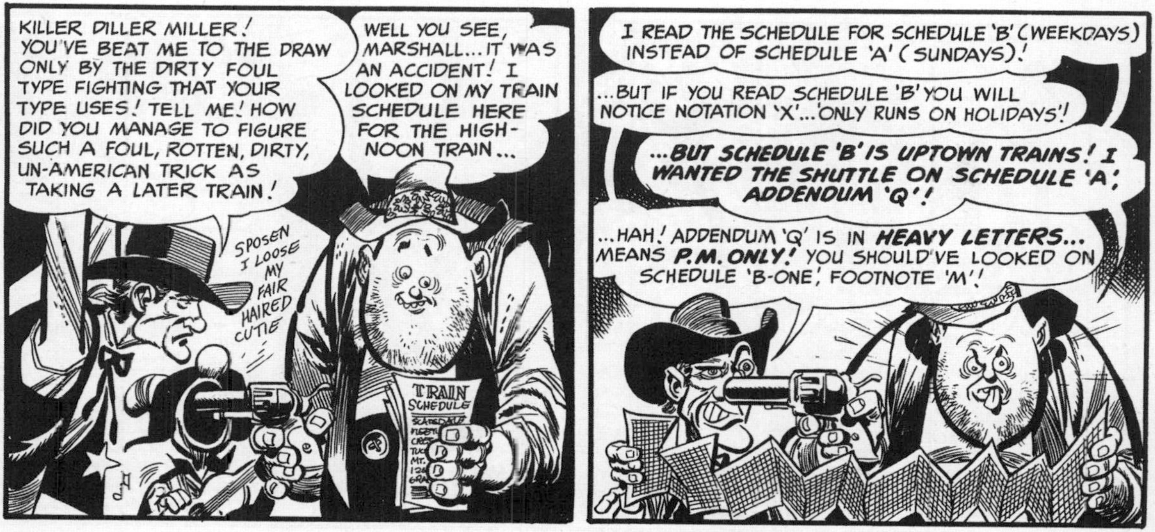
KILLER DILLER MILLER! YOU'VE BEAT ME TO THE DRAW ONLY BY THE DIRTY FOUL TYPE FIGHTING THAT YOUR TYPE USES! TELL ME! HOW DID YOU MANAGE TO FIGURE SUCH A FOUL, ROTTEN, DIRTY, UN-AMERICAN TRICK AS TAKING A LATER TRAIN!
WELL YOU SEE, MARSHALL... IT WAS AN ACCIDENT! I LOOKED ON MY TRAIN SCHEDULE HERE FOR THE HIGH-NOON TRAIN...
SPOSEN I LOOSE MY FAIR HAIRED CUTIE
TRAIN SCHEDULE
I READ THE SCHEDULE FOR SCHEDULE 'B' (WEEKDAYS) INSTEAD OF SCHEDULE 'A' (SUNDAYS)!
...BUT IF YOU READ SCHEDULE 'B' YOU WILL NOTICE NOTATION 'X'... 'ONLY RUNS ON HOLIDAYS'!
...**BUT SCHEDULE 'B' IS UPTOWN TRAINS! I WANTED THE SHUTTLE ON SCHEDULE 'A', ADDENDUM 'Q'!**
...HAH! ADDENDUM 'Q' IS IN **HEAVY LETTERS...** MEANS **P.M. ONLY!** YOU SHOULD'VE LOOKED ON SCHEDULE 'B-ONE', FOOTNOTE 'M'!

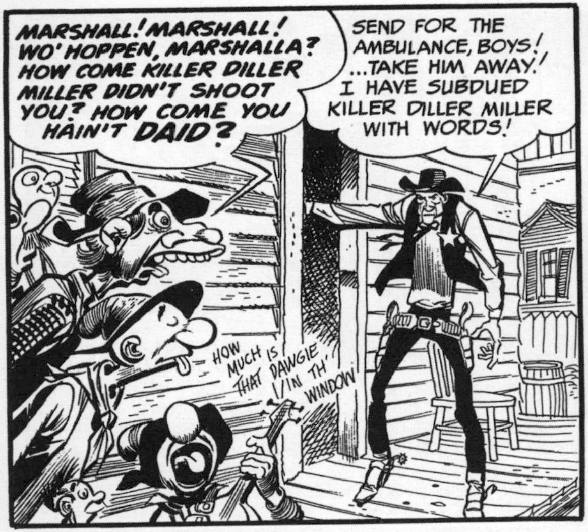
MARSHALL! MARSHALL! WO' HOPPEN, MARSHALLA? HOW COME KILLER DILLER MILLER DIDN'T SHOOT YOU? HOW COME YOU HAIN'T DAID?
SEND FOR THE AMBULANCE, BOYS! ...TAKE HIM AWAY! I HAVE SUBDUED KILLER DILLER MILLER WITH WORDS!
HOW MUCH IS THAT DAWGIE IN TH' WINDOW

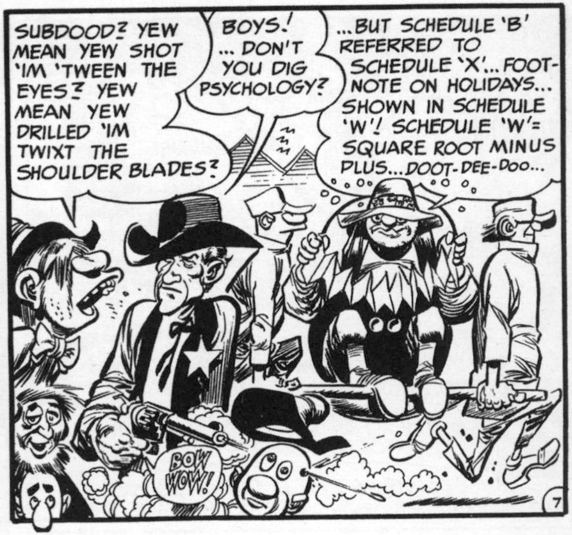
SUBDOOD? YEW MEAN YEW SHOT 'IM 'TWEEN THE EYES? YEW MEAN YEW DRILLED 'IM TWIXT THE SHOULDER BLADES?
BOYS! ... DON'T YOU DIG PSYCHOLOGY?
...BUT SCHEDULE 'B' REFERRED TO SCHEDULE 'X'... FOOT-NOTE ON HOLIDAYS... SHOWN IN SCHEDULE 'W'! SCHEDULE 'W'= SQUARE ROOT MINUS PLUS... DOOT-DEE-DOO...
BOW WOW!
7

SCENES WE'D LIKE TO SEE

DEPT. II:

The Musketeer Who Failed To Get The Girl.

122

REPORT FROM AMERICA DEPT: IN LINE WITH OUR POLICY OF KEEPING READERS OFF BALANCE, WE PRESENT HERE A SPECIAL FEATURE ON ANOTHER SERIOUS SUBJECT . . . FAMILY LIFE IN AMERICA . . . LIKE FOR INSTANCE THE OLD INSTITUTION OF THE SUNDAY AFTERNOON, WHEN DAD DECIDES TO TAKE THE FAMILY TO A . . .

RESTAURANT!

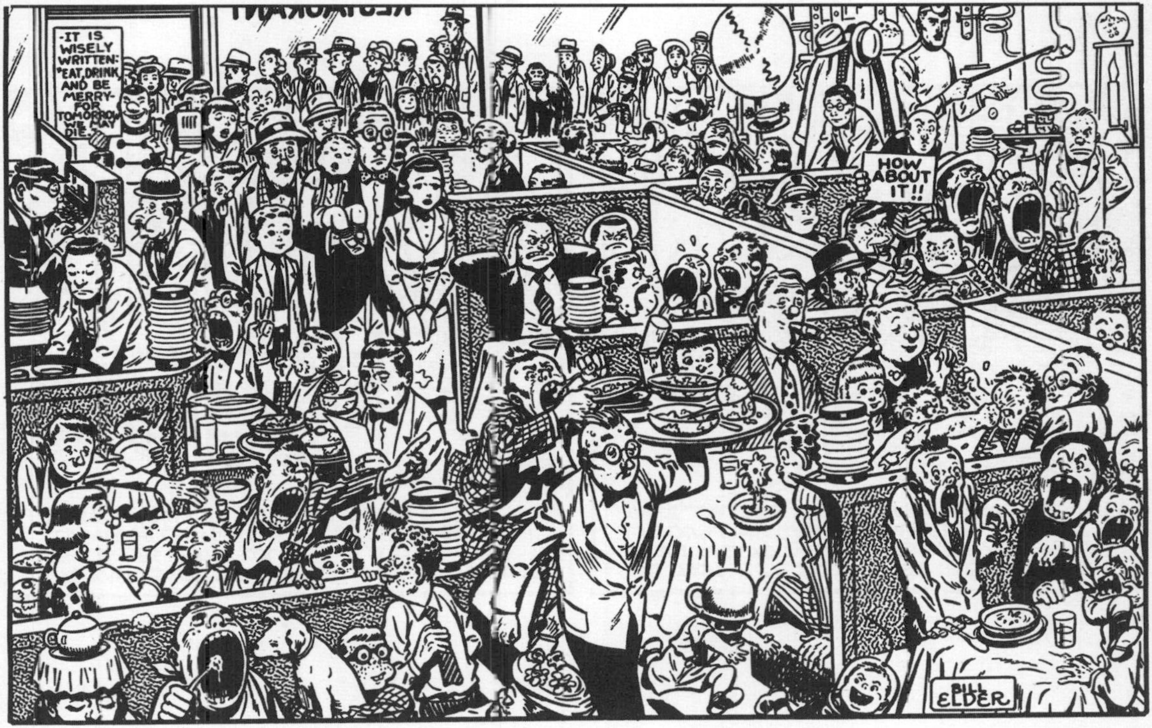
-IT IS WISELY WRITTEN: "EAT, DRINK AND BE MERRY- FOR TOMORROW WE MAY DIE."
HOW ABOUT IT!!
BILL ELDER

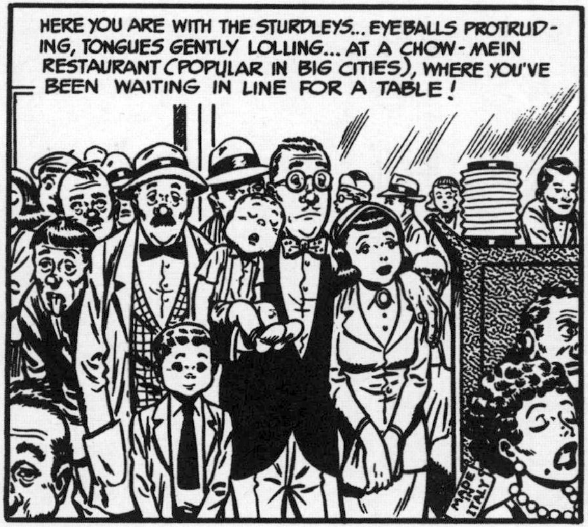
HERE YOU ARE WITH THE STURDLEYS... EYEBALLS PROTRUDING, TONGUES GENTLY LOLLING... AT A CHOW-MEIN RESTAURANT (POPULAR IN BIG CITIES), WHERE YOU'VE BEEN WAITING IN LINE FOR A TABLE!
MADE IN ITALY

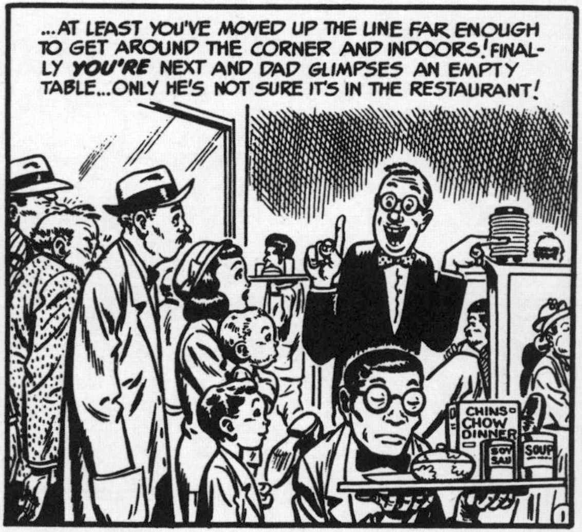
...AT LEAST YOU'VE MOVED UP THE LINE FAR ENOUGH TO GET AROUND THE CORNER AND INDOORS! FINALLY *YOU'RE* NEXT AND DAD GLIMPSES AN EMPTY TABLE...ONLY HE'S NOT SURE IT'S IN THE RESTAURANT!
CHINS CHOW DINNER
SOY SAU
SOUP

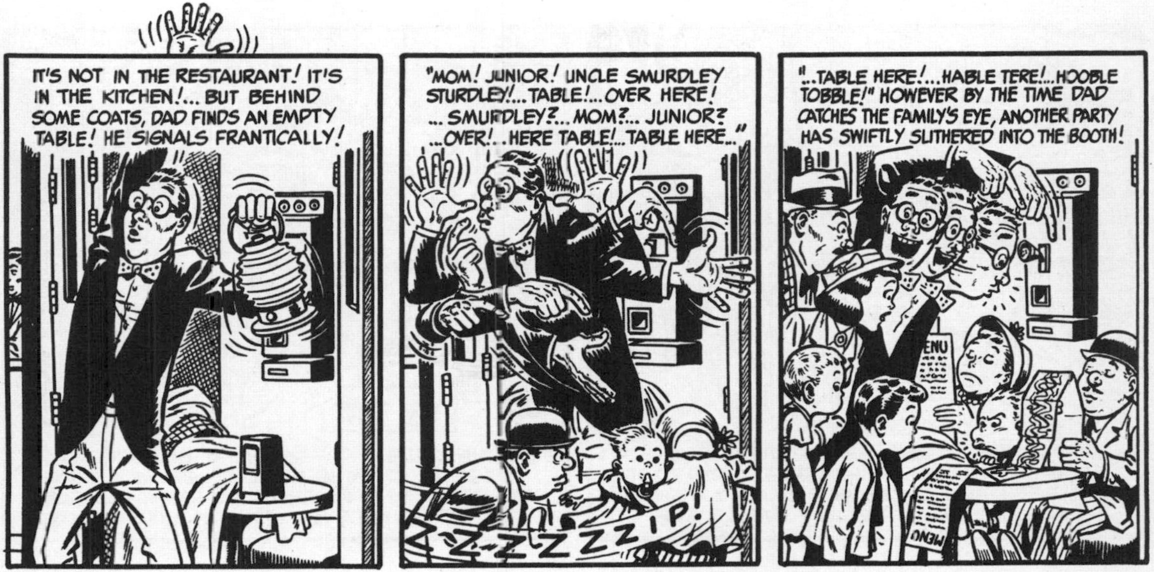
IT'S NOT IN THE RESTAURANT! IT'S IN THE KITCHEN!... BUT BEHIND SOME COATS, DAD FINDS AN EMPTY TABLE! HE SIGNALS FRANTICALLY!
"MOM! JUNIOR! UNCLE SMURDLEY STURDLEY!... TABLE!... OVER HERE! ... SMURDLEY?... MOM?... JUNIOR? ...OVER!.. HERE TABLE!... TABLE HERE..."
Z-Z-ZZZZZZIP!
"...TABLE HERE!... HABLE TERE!... HOOBLE TOBBLE!" HOWEVER BY THE TIME DAD CATCHES THE FAMILY'S EYE, ANOTHER PARTY HAS SWIFTLY SLITHERED INTO THE BOOTH!
MENU
MENU

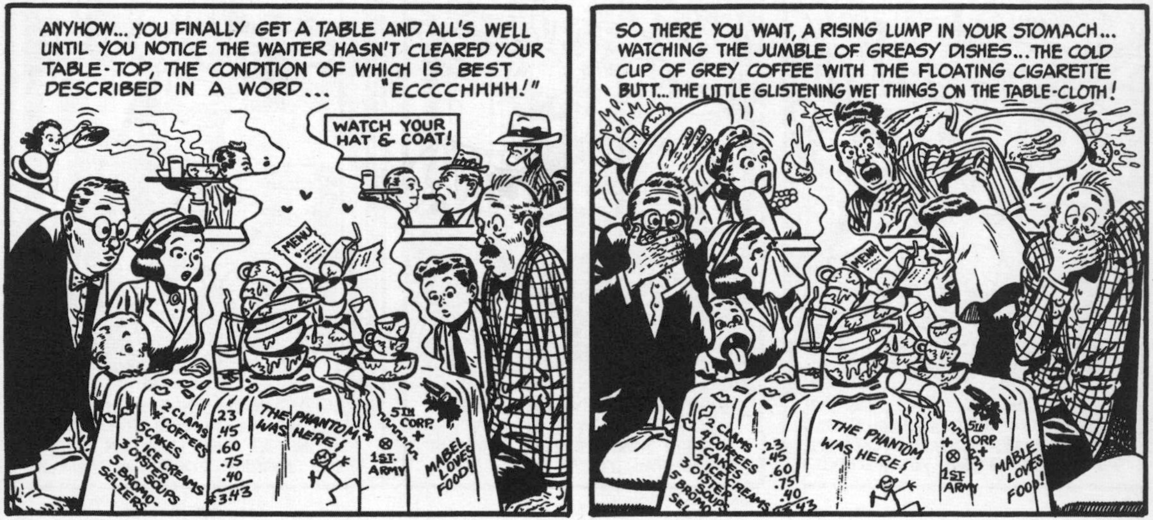
ANYHOW... YOU FINALLY GET A TABLE AND ALL'S WELL UNTIL YOU NOTICE THE WAITER HASN'T CLEARED YOUR TABLE-TOP, THE CONDITION OF WHICH IS BEST DESCRIBED IN A WORD... "ECCCCHHHH!"
WATCH YOUR HAT & COAT!
MENU
2 CLAMS .23
4 COFFEES .45
5 CAKES .60
2 ICE CREAMS .75
3 OYSTER SOUPS .40
5 BROMO-SELTZERS
$3.43
THE PHANTOM WAS HERE!
5TH CORP.
1ST. ARMY
MABEL LOVES FOOD!
SO THERE YOU WAIT, A RISING LUMP IN YOUR STOMACH... WATCHING THE JUMBLE OF GREASY DISHES... THE COLD CUP OF GREY COFFEE WITH THE FLOATING CIGARETTE BUTT... THE LITTLE GLISTENING WET THINGS ON THE TABLE-CLOTH!
MENU
THE PHANTOM WAS HERE!
MABLE LOVES FOOD!

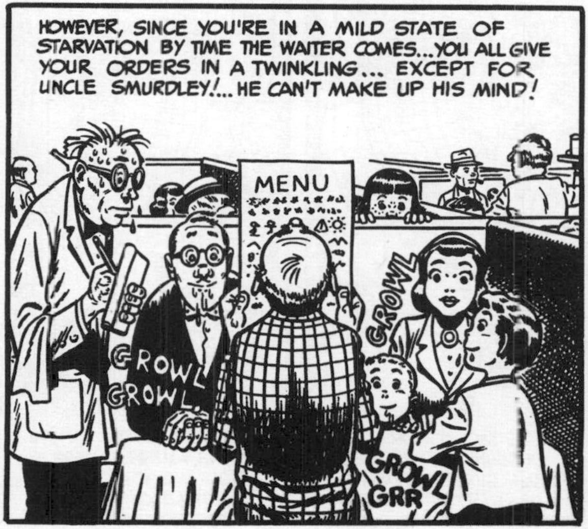
HOWEVER, SINCE YOU'RE IN A MILD STATE OF STARVATION BY TIME THE WAITER COMES...YOU ALL GIVE YOUR ORDERS IN A TWINKLING... EXCEPT FOR UNCLE SMURDLEY!... HE CAN'T MAKE UP HIS MIND!
MENU
GROWL GROWL
GROWL
GROWL GRR

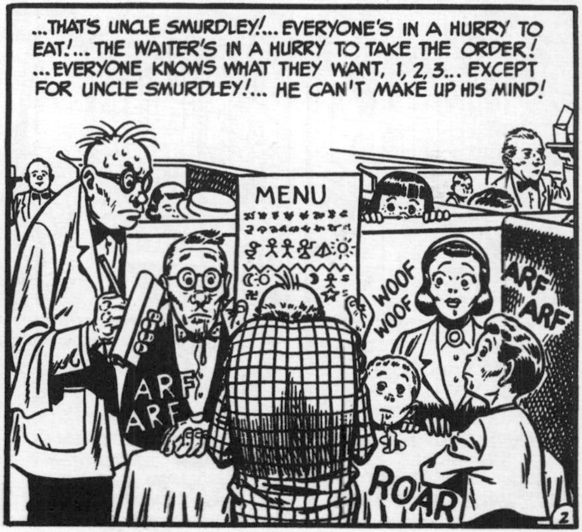
...THAT'S UNCLE SMURDLEY!... EVERYONE'S IN A HURRY TO EAT!... THE WAITER'S IN A HURRY TO TAKE THE ORDER! ...EVERYONE KNOWS WHAT THEY WANT, 1, 2, 3... EXCEPT FOR UNCLE SMURDLEY!... HE CAN'T MAKE UP HIS MIND!
MENU
WOOF WOOF
ARF ARF
ARF ARF
ROAR
2

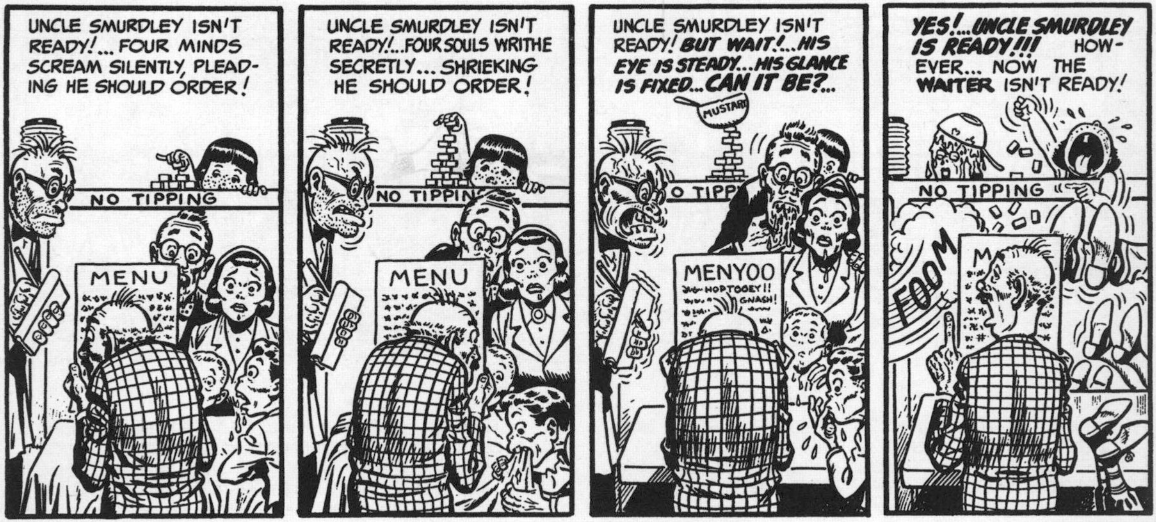
UNCLE SMURDLEY ISN'T READY!... FOUR MINDS SCREAM SILENTLY, PLEADING HE SHOULD ORDER!
NO TIPPING
MENU
UNCLE SMURDLEY ISN'T READY!...FOUR SOULS WRITHE SECRETLY... SHRIEKING HE SHOULD ORDER!
NO TIPPIN
MENU
UNCLE SMURDLEY ISN'T READY! BUT WAIT!...HIS EYE IS STEADY...HIS GLANCE IS FIXED...CAN IT BE?...
MUSTARD
O TIPP
MENYOO
HOPTOOEY!!
GNASH!
YES!...UNCLE SMURDLEY IS READY!!! HOW-EVER... NOW THE WAITER ISN'T READY!
NO TIPPING
FOOM

EVENTUALLY, YOU DO GET FOOD!... AND THE WAY IT'S SERVED...YOU REALLY GET A TERRIFIC APPETITE JUST LOOKING!...ON FRESH WHITE LINEN, AMIDST SHINY SILVERWARE STILL WARM FROM A SCALDING BATH...

...BOWLS OF THICK STEAMING SOUP...GLEAMING COVERED PORCELAIN CASSEROLES EXUDING FRAGRANCE... TASTY SAUCES ON LITTLE DISHES HOT FROM THE KITCHEN...BOY! WOULD YOU GET SICK IF YOU SAW THE KITCHEN!
IN
JOE'S GARAGE
SHORT ORDER COOK

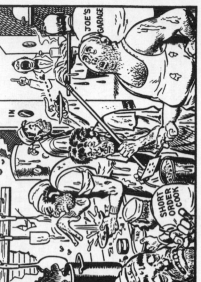

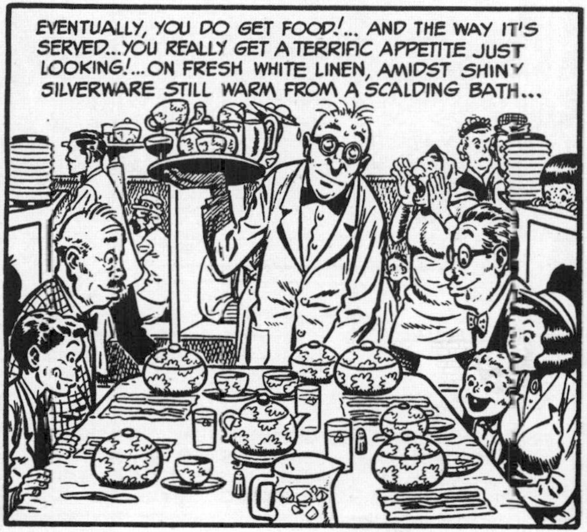

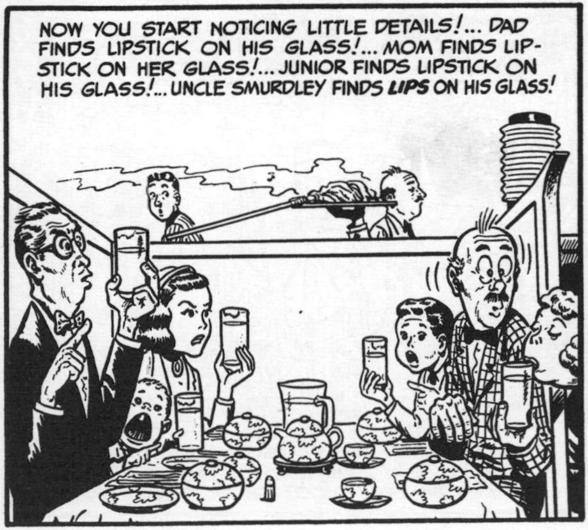
NOW YOU START NOTICING LITTLE DETAILS!... DAD FINDS LIPSTICK ON HIS GLASS!... MOM FINDS LIPSTICK ON HER GLASS!... JUNIOR FINDS LIPSTICK ON HIS GLASS!... UNCLE SMURDLEY FINDS **LIPS** ON HIS GLASS!

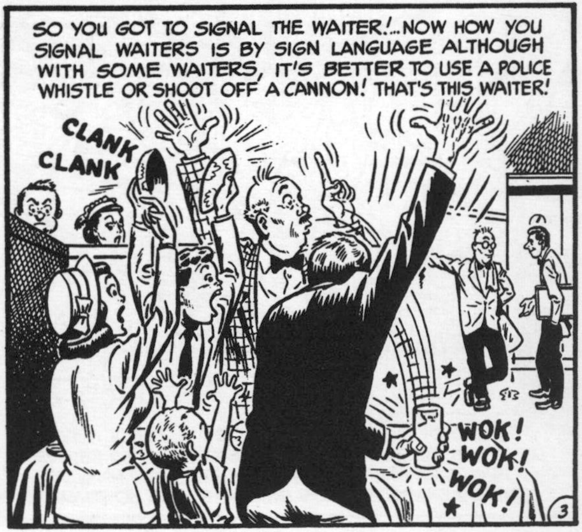
SO YOU GOT TO SIGNAL THE WAITER!...NOW HOW YOU SIGNAL WAITERS IS BY SIGN LANGUAGE ALTHOUGH WITH SOME WAITERS, IT'S BETTER TO USE A POLICE WHISTLE OR SHOOT OFF A CANNON! THAT'S THIS WAITER!
CLANK
CLANK
WOK!
WOK!
WOK!
3

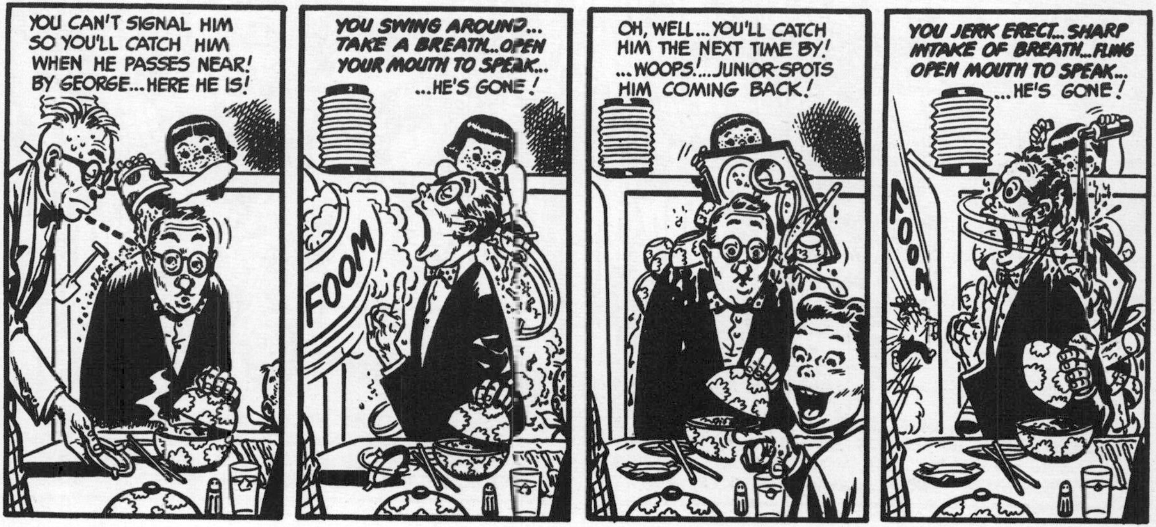
YOU CAN'T SIGNAL HIM SO YOU'LL CATCH HIM WHEN HE PASSES NEAR! BY GEORGE...HERE HE IS!
YOU SWING AROUND... TAKE A BREATH...OPEN YOUR MOUTH TO SPEAK... ...HE'S GONE!
FOOM
OH, WELL...YOU'LL CATCH HIM THE NEXT TIME BY! ...WOOPS!...JUNIOR SPOTS HIM COMING BACK!
YOU JERK ERECT...SHARP INTAKE OF BREATH...FLING OPEN MOUTH TO SPEAK... ...HE'S GONE!
FOOM

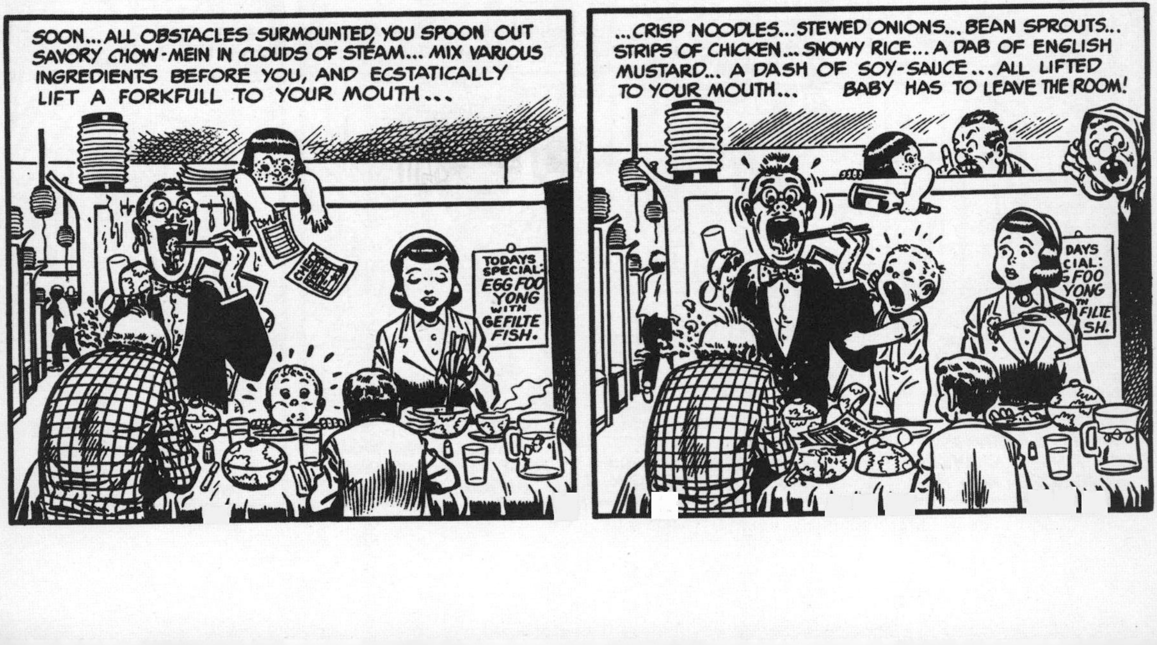
SOON...ALL OBSTACLES SURMOUNTED, YOU SPOON OUT SAVORY CHOW-MEIN IN CLOUDS OF STEAM... MIX VARIOUS INGREDIENTS BEFORE YOU, AND ECSTATICALLY LIFT A FORKFULL TO YOUR MOUTH...
TODAYS SPECIAL: EGG FOO YONG WITH GEFILTE FISH.
CHECK
...CRISP NOODLES...STEWED ONIONS... BEAN SPROUTS... STRIPS OF CHICKEN... SNOWY RICE... A DAB OF ENGLISH MUSTARD... A DASH OF SOY-SAUCE... ALL LIFTED TO YOUR MOUTH...
BABY HAS TO LEAVE THE ROOM!
CHECK

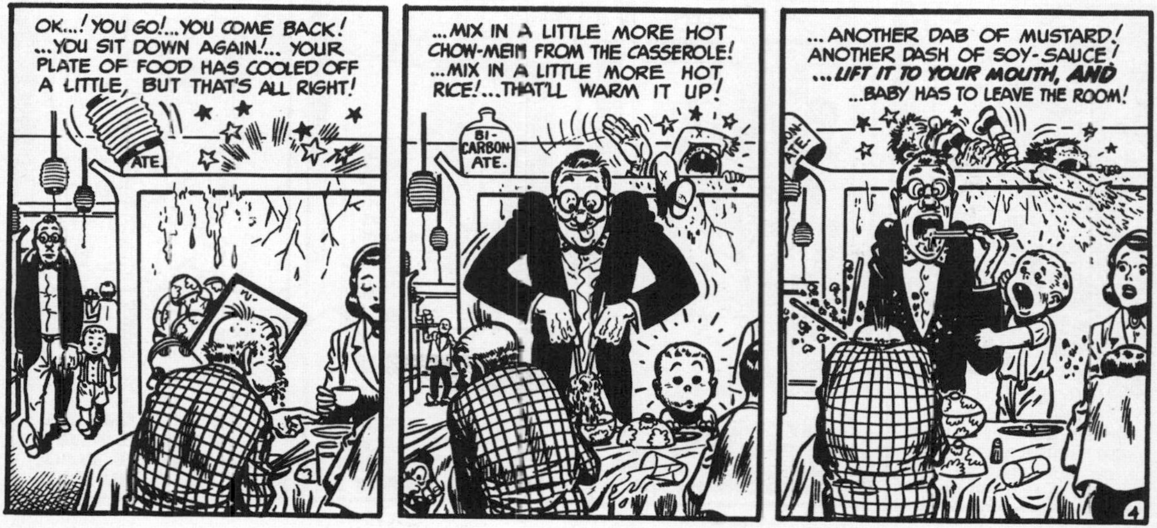
OK...! YOU GO!...YOU COME BACK! ...YOU SIT DOWN AGAIN!... YOUR PLATE OF FOOD HAS COOLED OFF A LITTLE, BUT THAT'S ALL RIGHT!
ATE.
...MIX IN A LITTLE MORE HOT CHOW-MEIN FROM THE CASSEROLE! ...MIX IN A LITTLE MORE HOT RICE!...THAT'LL WARM IT UP!
BI-CARBON-ATE.
...ANOTHER DAB OF MUSTARD! ANOTHER DASH OF SOY-SAUCE! ...***LIFT IT TO YOUR MOUTH, AND*** ...BABY HAS TO LEAVE THE ROOM!
4

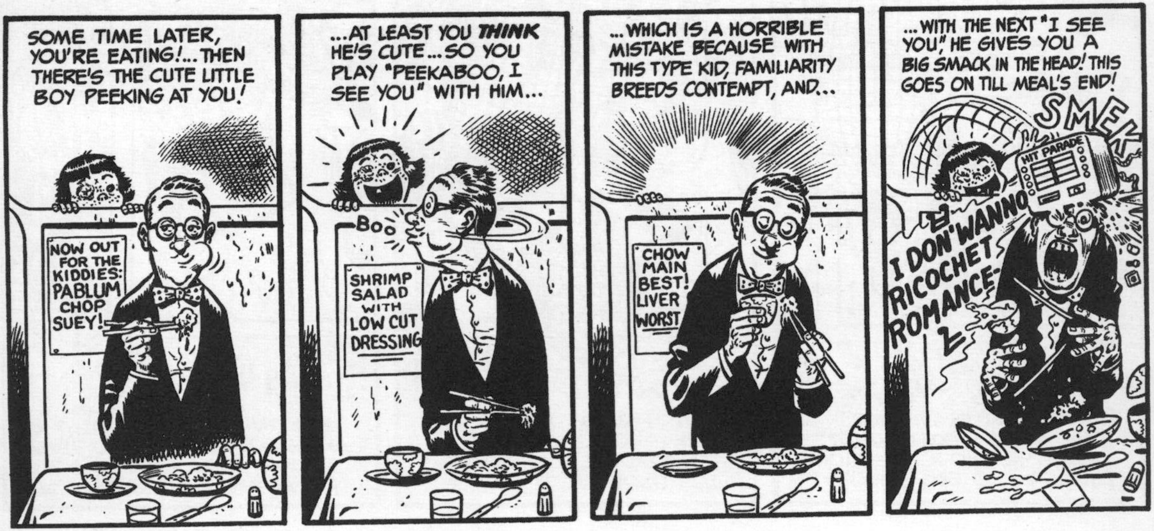
SOME TIME LATER, YOU'RE EATING!... THEN THERE'S THE CUTE LITTLE BOY PEEKING AT YOU!
NOW OUT FOR THE KIDDIES: PABLUM CHOP SUEY!
...AT LEAST YOU *THINK* HE'S CUTE... SO YOU PLAY "PEEKABOO, I SEE YOU" WITH HIM...
BOO
SHRIMP SALAD WITH LOW CUT DRESSING
... WHICH IS A HORRIBLE MISTAKE BECAUSE WITH THIS TYPE KID, FAMILIARITY BREEDS CONTEMPT, AND...
CHOW MAIN BEST! LIVER WORST
...WITH THE NEXT "I SEE YOU," HE GIVES YOU A BIG SMACK IN THE HEAD! THIS GOES ON TILL MEAL'S END!
SMEK
HIT PARADE
I DON' WANNO RICOCHET ROMANCE

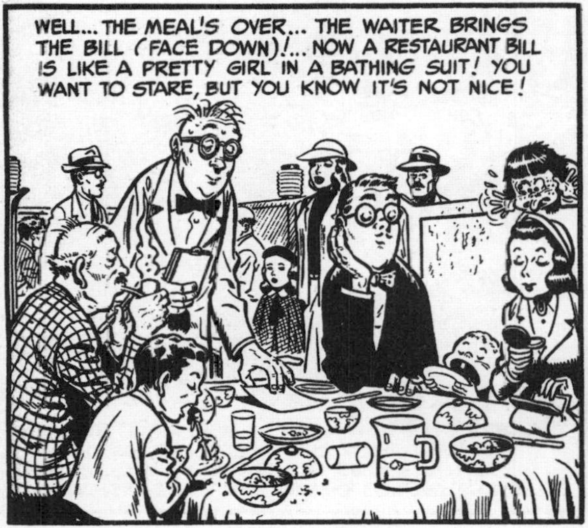
WELL... THE MEAL'S OVER... THE WAITER BRINGS THE BILL (FACE DOWN)!... NOW A RESTAURANT BILL IS LIKE A PRETTY GIRL IN A BATHING SUIT! YOU WANT TO STARE, BUT YOU KNOW IT'S NOT NICE!

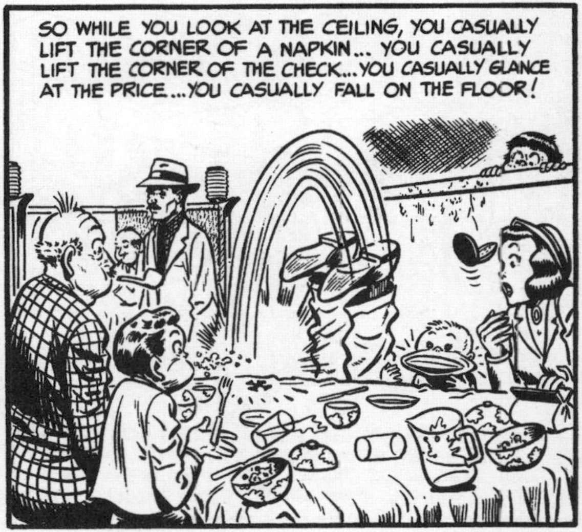
SO WHILE YOU LOOK AT THE CEILING, YOU CASUALLY LIFT THE CORNER OF A NAPKIN... YOU CASUALLY LIFT THE CORNER OF THE CHECK...YOU CASUALLY GLANCE AT THE PRICE...YOU CASUALLY FALL ON THE FLOOR!

ALTHOUGH PEOPLE ARE WAITING FOR TABLES, YOU WANT TO SIT A MOMENT TO SMOKE...TO LET THE FOOD SETTLE! THE WAITER TAKES AWAY THE DISHES...TAKES AWAY THE ASH-TRAY... THE TABLE CLOTH...

BUT WHEN THE WAITER TAKES AWAY THE TABLE AND WHEN THE PEOPLE START SITTING DOWN NEXT TO YOU AND START TUCKING NAPKINS UNDER THEIR CHINS, YOU FIGURE MAYBE THEY WANT YOU TO LEAVE!

THE TIP!... UNCLE SMURDLEY DIGS FOR HIS COAT... YOU DIG FOR THE TIP!... YOU ACT UN-CONCERNED...DEVIL-MAY-CARE
HOWEVER, INSIDE... YOUR MIND RACES FURIOUSLY... CALCULATING! YOU PUT DOWN THE TIP AND RUN IN SHAME BEFORE THE WAITER COMES!
HALF-WAY OUT THE DOOR, YOUR CON-SCIENCE STOPS YOU!...YOU DON'T WANT TO LOOK CHEAP! YOU RUN BACK AND PUT DOWN A FEW MORE COINS!

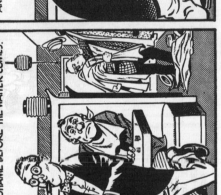

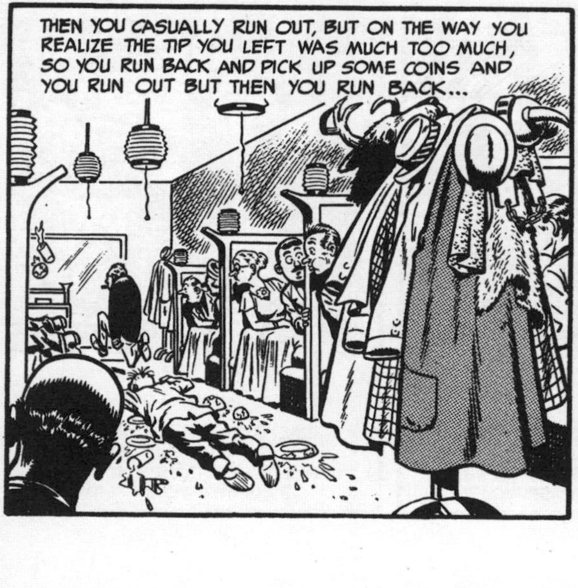
THEN YOU CASUALLY RUN OUT, BUT ON THE WAY YOU REALIZE THE TIP YOU LEFT WAS MUCH TOO MUCH, SO YOU RUN BACK AND PICK UP SOME COINS AND YOU RUN OUT BUT THEN YOU RUN BACK...

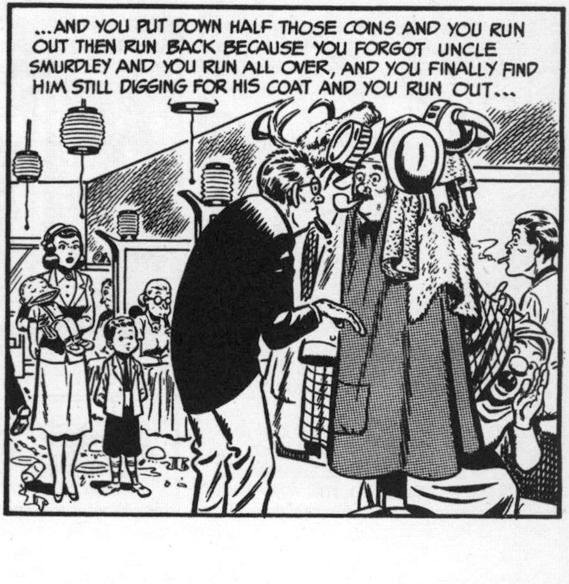
...AND YOU PUT DOWN HALF THOSE COINS AND YOU RUN OUT THEN RUN BACK BECAUSE YOU FORGOT UNCLE SMURDLEY AND YOU RUN ALL OVER, AND YOU FINALLY FIND HIM STILL DIGGING FOR HIS COAT AND YOU RUN OUT...

...HERE YOU ARE WITH THE STURDLEYS...EYEBALLS PRO-TRUDING, TONGUES GENTLY LOLLING...AT A CHOW-MEIN RESTAURANT (POPULAR IN BIG CITIES) WHERE YOU'VE BEEN WAITING IN LINE FOR A TABLE...

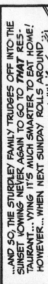

...AND SO, THE STURDLEY FAMILY TRUDGES OFF INTO THE SUNSET VOWING NEVER AGAIN TO GO TO *THAT* RES-TAURANT... VYING IT'S MUCH SMARTER TO EAT HOME! HOWEVER... WHEN NEXT SUNDAY ROLLS AROUND...

CHAIN STORE

SALE

FEN MEN CHEW RESTAURANT

POETRY DEPT.: WE'VE GIVEN YOU A LITTLE OF EVERYTHING IN THIS BOOK . . . EVERYTHING TO KEEP YOU FROM FALLING ASLEEP . . . HORROR, WESTERNS, MEDICINE, NOW POETRY; EVEN THAT! . . . A POEM YOU'VE NO DOUBT HEARD OF, NAME OF . . .

CASEY AT THE BAT!

BY ERNEST LAWRENCE THAYER

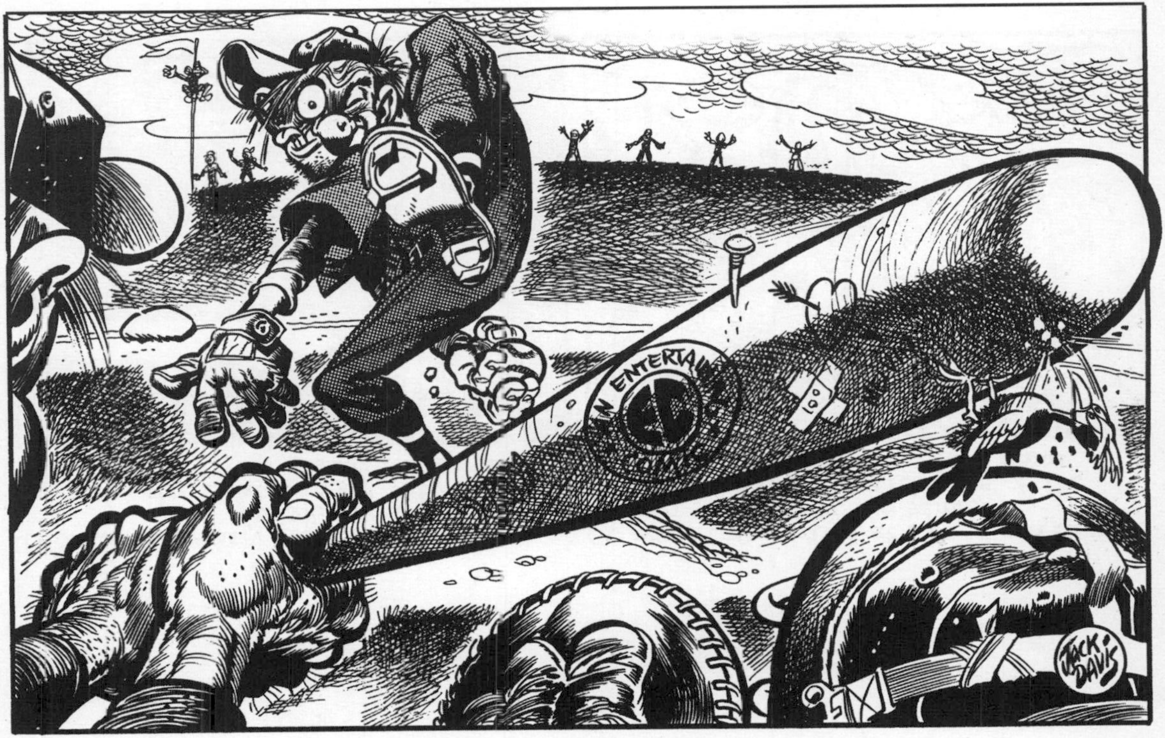
JACK DAVIS

It looked extremely rocky for the
Mudville nine that day;
The score stood two to four with but
one inning left to play.

So when Cooney died at second and Burrows
did the same,
A pallor wreathed the features of the
patrons of the game.

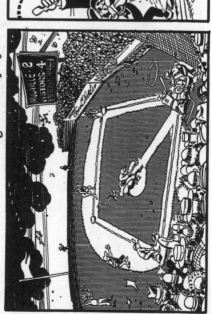

The straggling few got up to go, leaving there the rest,
With the hope that springs eternal within the human breast.

For they thought: "If only Casey could get a whack at that,"
They'd put even money now, with Casey at the bat.

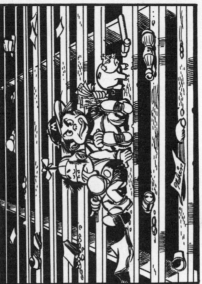

144

But Flynn preceded Casey, and likewise
    so did Blake,
And the former was a pudd'n, and the latter
    was a fake.

So on that stricken multitude a deathlike
    silence sat;
For there seemed but little chance for Casey's
    getting to the bat.

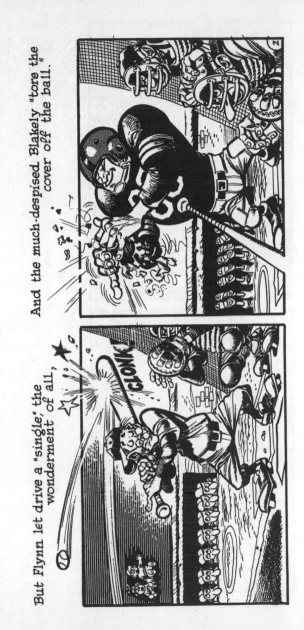

But Flynn let drive a "single," the wonderment of all,

And the much-despised Blakely "tore the cover off the ball."

And when the dust had lifted, and
they saw what had occurred,

There was Blakely safe at second, and
Flynn a-huggin' third.

Then from the gladdened multitude
went up a joyous yell —
It rumbled in the mountaintops, it rattled
in the dell;

It struck upon the hillside and rebounded
on the flat;
For Casey, mighty Casey, was advancing
to the bat.

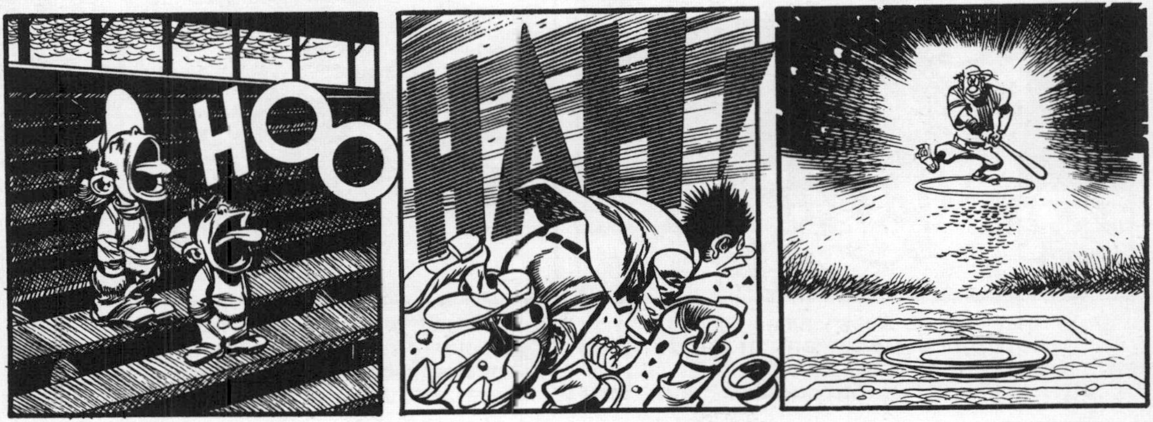
HOO
HAH

There was *ease* in Casey's manner as
he stepped into his place,
There was *pride* in Casey's bearing and a
smile on Casey's face;

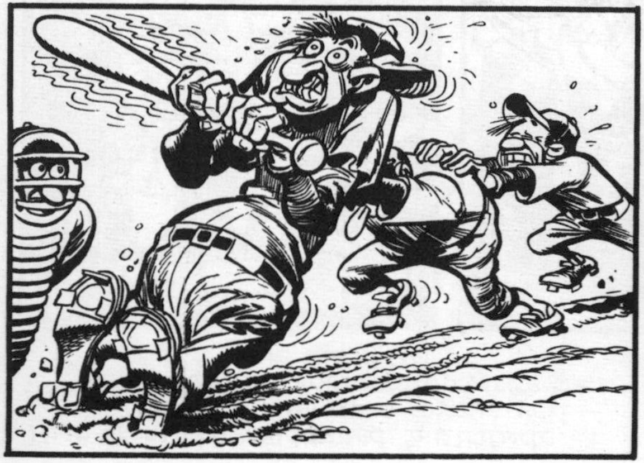

And when responding to the cheers, he
lightly doffed his hat,
No stranger in the crowd could doubt
'twas Casey at the bat.

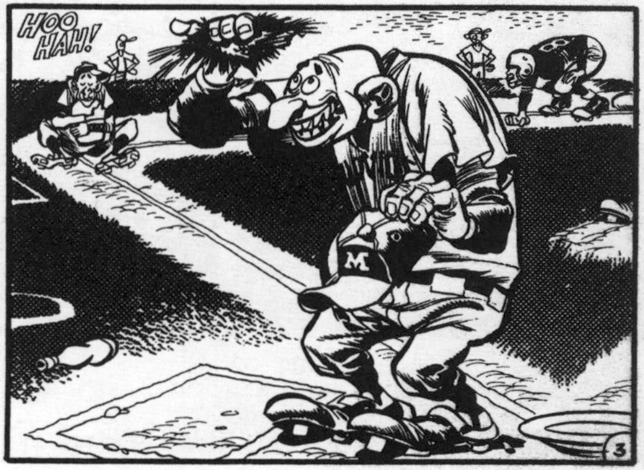
HOO HAH!
3

Ten thousand eyes were on him as he rubbed his hands with dirt.

Five thousand tongues applauded when he wiped them on his shirt;

Then when the writhing pitcher ground the
    ball into his hip,
Defiance gleamed in Casey's eye, a sneer
    curled Casey's lip.

And now the leather-covered sphere came
    hurtling through the air,
And Casey stood a-watching it in haughty
    grandeur there.

Close by the sturdy batsman the ball
unheeded sped.
"That ain't my style," said Casey. "Strike one,"
the umpire said.

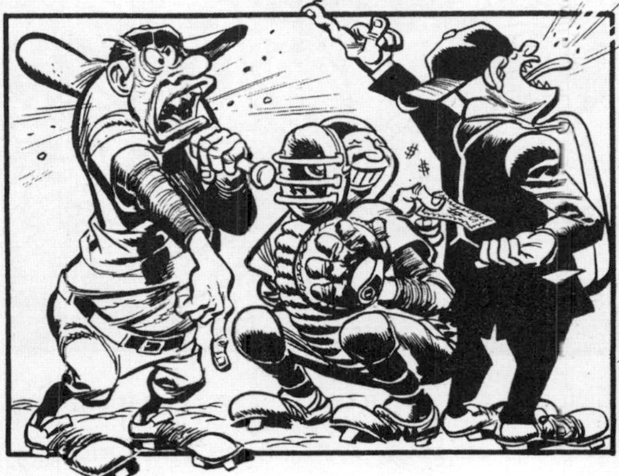

From the benches, black with people, there went
up a muffled roar,
Like the beating of the storm waves on the
stern and distant shore.

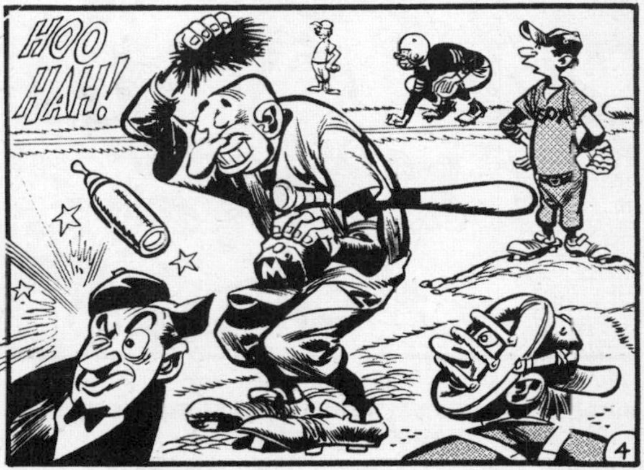
HOO HAH!
4

"Kill him! Kill the umpire!" someone shouted in the stand;
And it's likely they'd have killed him had not Casey raised his hand.

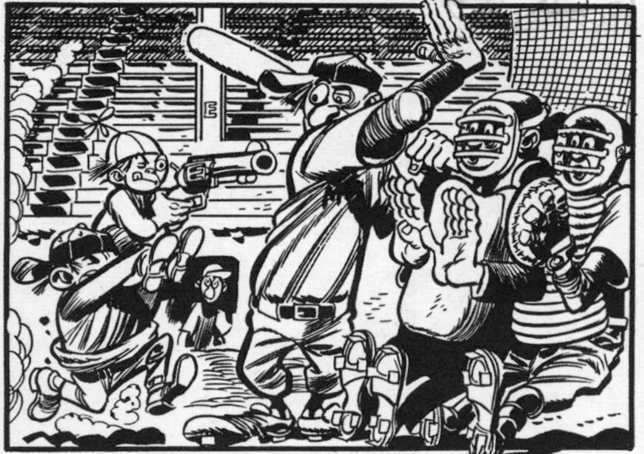

With a smile of Christian charity great Casey's visage shone;
He stilled the rising tumult, he made the game go on;

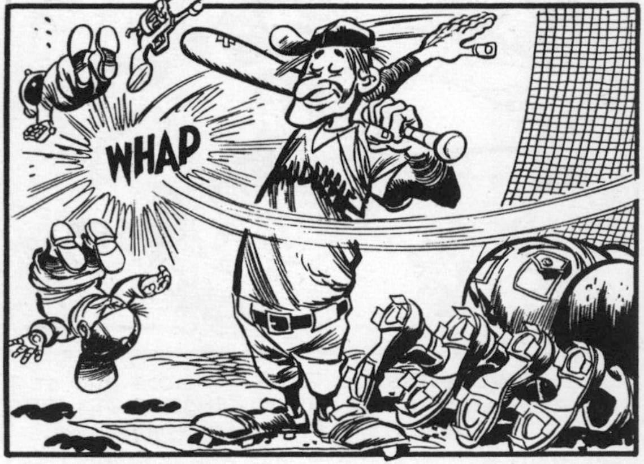
WHAP

He signaled to the pitcher, and once more
the spheroid flew;
But Casey still ignored it, and the umpire said,
"Strike two."

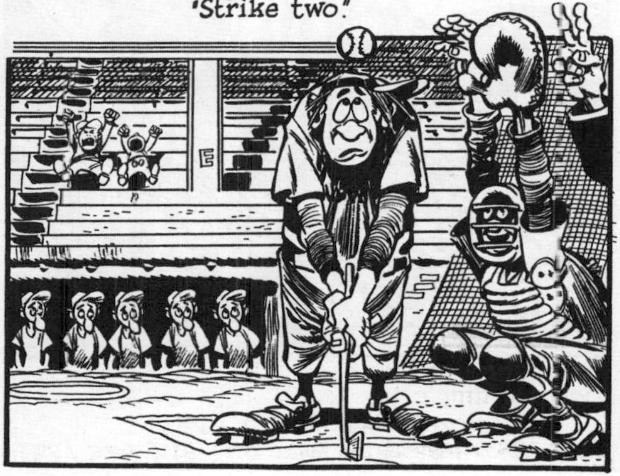

"Fraud!" cried the maddened thousands, and
the echo answered "Fraud!"
But one scornful look from Casey and
the audience was awed;

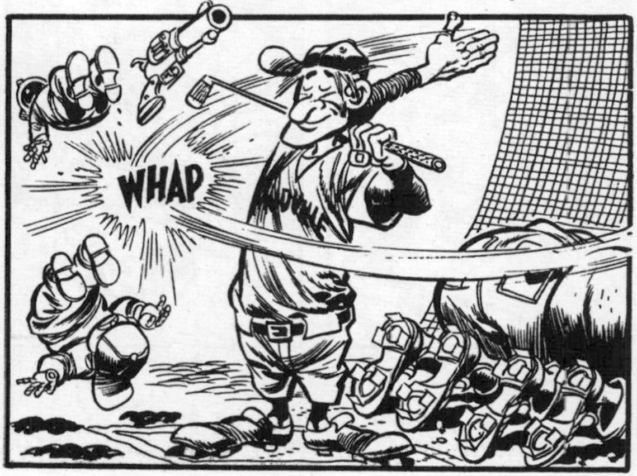
WHAP

They saw his face grow stern and cold, they saw his muscles strain,

And they knew, that Casey wouldn't let the ball go by again.

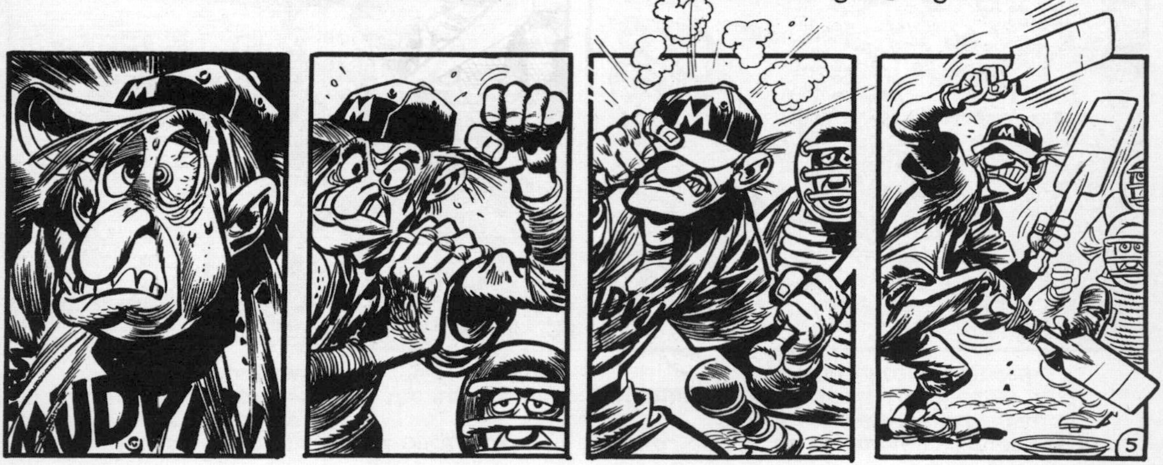

The sneer is gone from Casey's lips,
his teeth are clenched in hate,

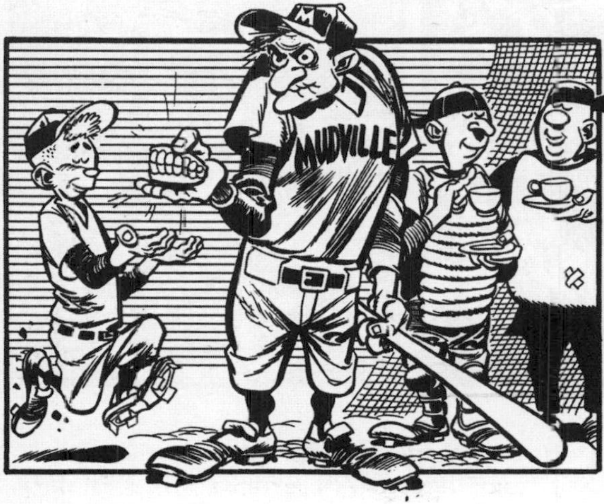
MUDVILLE

He pounds with cruel vengeance
his bat upon the plate;

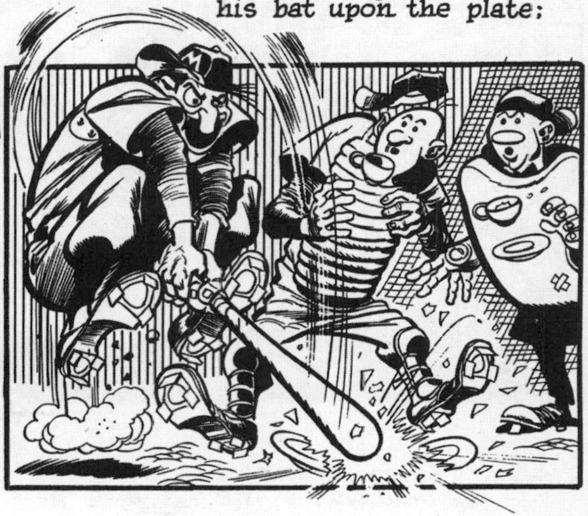

And now the pitcher holds the ball,
And now he lets it go.

And now the air is shattered by
the force of Casey's blow.

Oh, somewhere in this favored land the sun is shining bright,
The band is playing somewhere, and somewhere hearts are light;

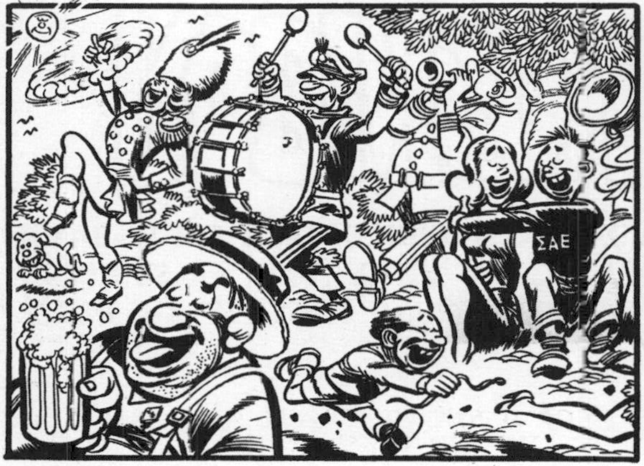
ΣΑΕ

And somewhere men are laughing, and somewhere children shout,
But there is no joy in Mudville — mighty Casey has struck out!

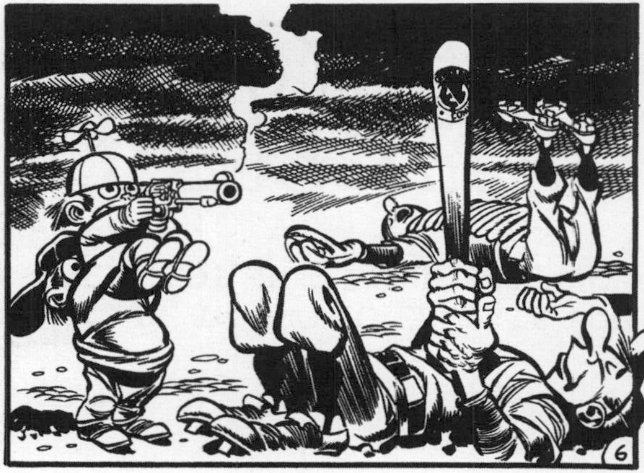

LITERARY CLASSICS DEPT: HERE WE GO AGAIN, TRYING TO EDUCATE YOU READERS . . . YOU TALK ABOUT THIS ONE A LOT, BUT WE'RE SURE YOU HAVEN'T READ IT, SO HERE IS OUR VERSION OF . . .

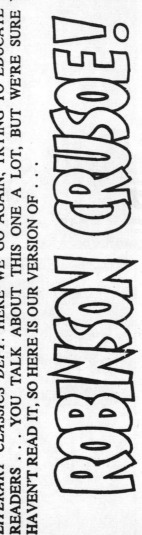

ROBINSON CRUSOE!

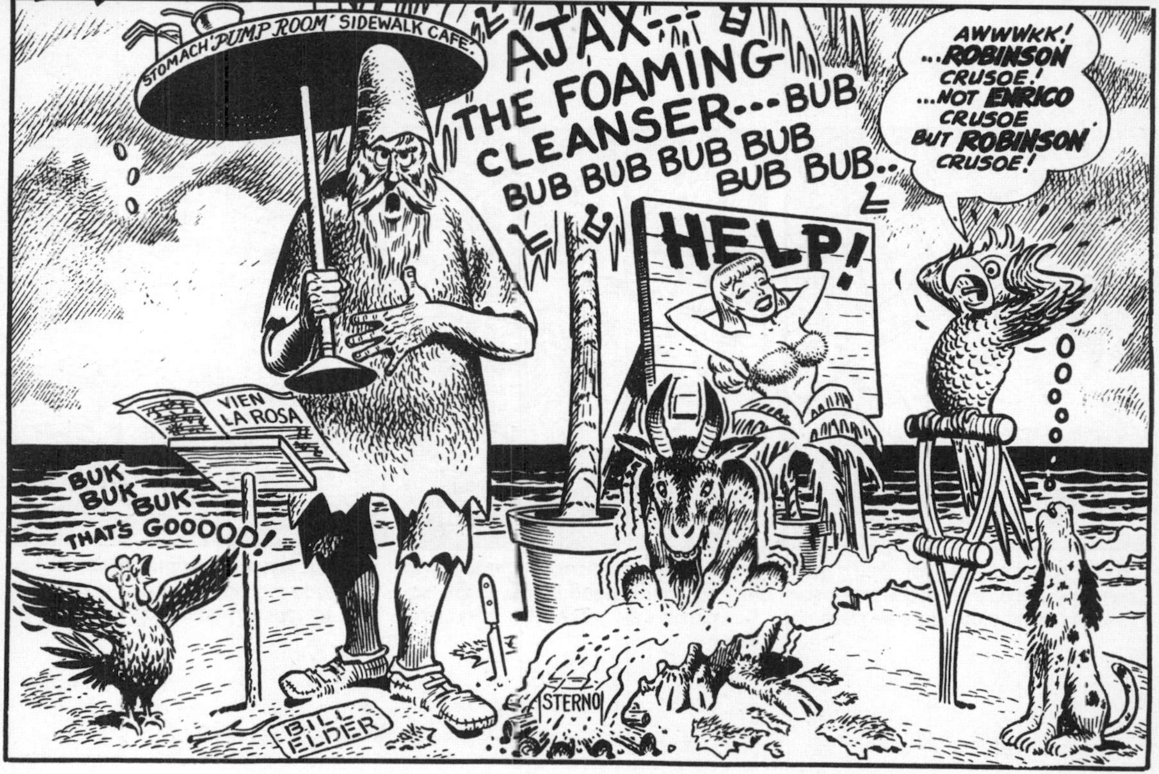
STOMACH 'PUMP ROOM' SIDEWALK CAFE
AJAX... THE FOAMING CLEANSER... BUB BUB BUB BUB BUB BUB BUB..
HELP!
AWWWKK! ...ROBINSON CRUSOE! ...NOT ENRICO CRUSOE BUT ROBINSON CRUSOE!
VIEN LA ROSA
BUK BUK BUK THAT'S GOOOOOD!
STERNO
BILL ELDER

My name is Robinson Crusoe! In the year 1652, while sailing the ocean, I found myself suddenly in the water!

Although my vessel was sturdy enough, I was in great trouble because of the rough condition of the water!

You see, I was taking a bath below decks, and what with rocking of the boat, I had lost my cake of soap!

I finally left my bath...yes...I had my clothes on since it's not nice to be unclothed in a comic book as well as a movie! Imagine my surprise when I stepped out of the water...

MR. CHRISTIAN!

IN CASE OF FIRE BREAK GLASS!

...to find myself stepping into more water! Yes...the boat was sinking! Vainly I fought the monstrous waves...trying to find that furshlugginer soap!

TIDE

Seeing the outline of an island, I swam in that direction, not too eagerly, in order to save my strength!
For eagerness could weaken me and I was determined not to be too eager for eagerness was no good!
MR. CHRISTIAN!
ESTHER WILLIAMS
I wasn't gonna be eager! Not me, boy! Imagine my surprise when I found I had swum right over the island...

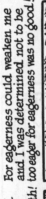

...the jagged rocky island! No wonder the water felt rough! I stood shakily on the shore of this wild island ...spent!... No money in my pockets... like I said... spent!

As I stood wondering how to stay alive, the storm abated and the water receded! You don't even have to imagine my surprise when I saw the ship...washed up on the rocks!

GOOD LUCK FLORENCE CHADWICK
MR. CHRISTIAN!
2

Without a moment's hesitation, I plunged into the surf! Without a moment's hesitation, I plunged out again! Brrr! It was cold! I then swam to the boat!

TEA
TO: BOSTON
MASS
U.S.A.
SEX
CRIME COMICS
DIRTY COMICS
PANIC
TEA
TO: BOSTON
MASS.
U.S.A.

Hoisting myself over the side, I found upon inspection, not a living soul aboard! Breaking into the storage locker, I found tools and a cask of rum!

P.F.C.
SIDNEY
POKHOLTZ
TALLAHASEE
FLORIDA
CPL.
CLYDE
SHAPIRO-
MONTANA
PVT.
TIMOTHY
TOMB.
COFFIN
CORNERS,
TEXAS
BOX
13.

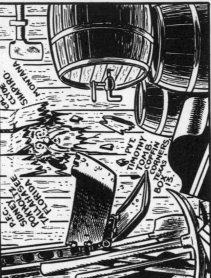

Determined to move the ship supplies to shore, I removed the tools, and... to bolster me, I took a cup of rum!
HOMES & GARDENS HANDYMAN'S GUIDE.
I then commenced cutting away lumber, which I threw over the side to fashion into a raft!
After lashing the lumber together, I was much fatigued and, to bolster me, I took another cup of rum!

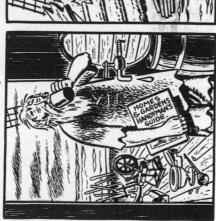

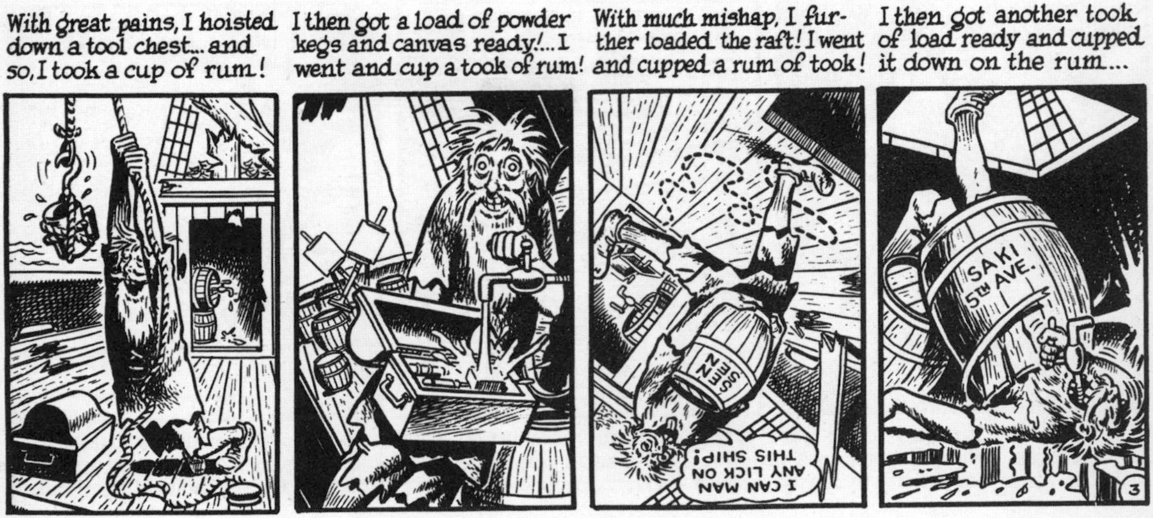
With great pains, I hoisted down a tool chest... and so, I took a cup of rum!
I then got a load of powder kegs and canvas ready!... I went and cup a took of rum!
With much mishap, I further loaded the raft! I went and cupped a rum of took!
SEN SEN
I CAN MAN ANY LICK ON THIS SHIP!
I then got another took of load ready and cupped it down on the rum...
SAKI 5TH AVE.

Boy! Was I drunk!... But the work had to be done, so I squared my shoulders, marched resolutely to my task... and fell overboard!...When I finally made my way to shore...

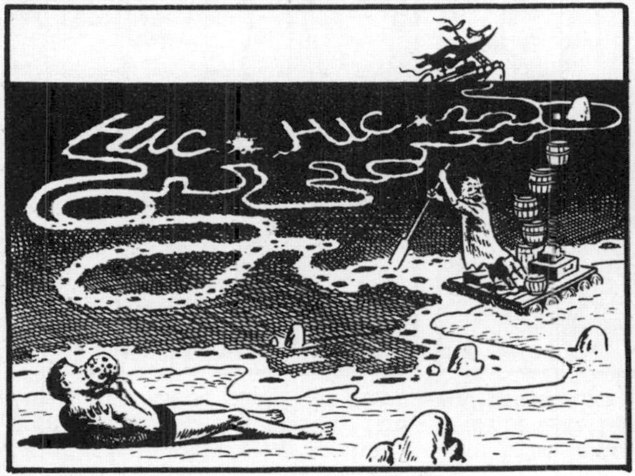
HIC HIC

...I sought immediately to protect myself and my supplies from wild beasts and savages! Choosing a cliff wall, I built a stockade snug against it!

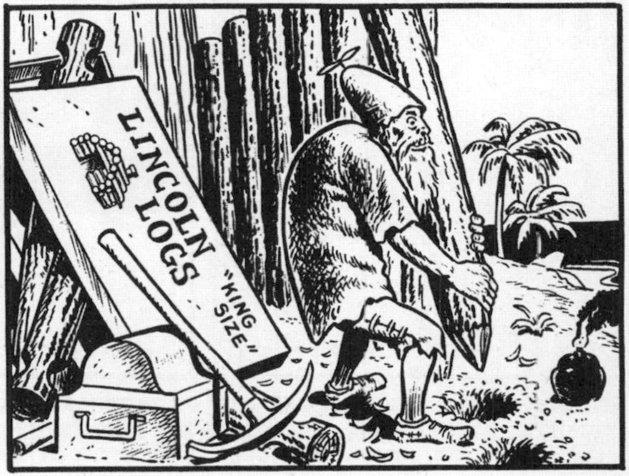
LINCOLN LOGS
"KING SIZE"

168

I built it high and strong so that nothing could get in, and too late I realized nothing could get out...

...for I had forgotten to build a door! However, I had all my tools and equipment and I made a ladder...

...and I got out...for man's ability to improvise...his ingenuity conquers all! Then it hit me!..How do I get in?

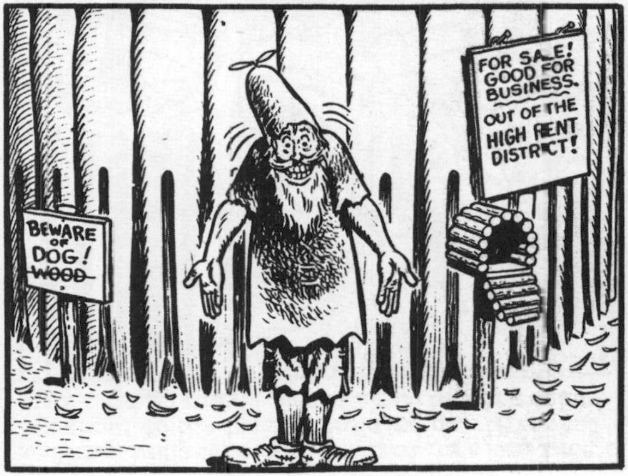
For the only way to climb the wall was with a ladder and the only ladder was inside the wall next to the only tools to make a ladder! Well...live and learn, I say!
BEWARE OF DOG! ~~WOOD~~
FOR SALE! GOOD FOR BUSINESS. OUT OF THE HIGH RENT DISTRICT!

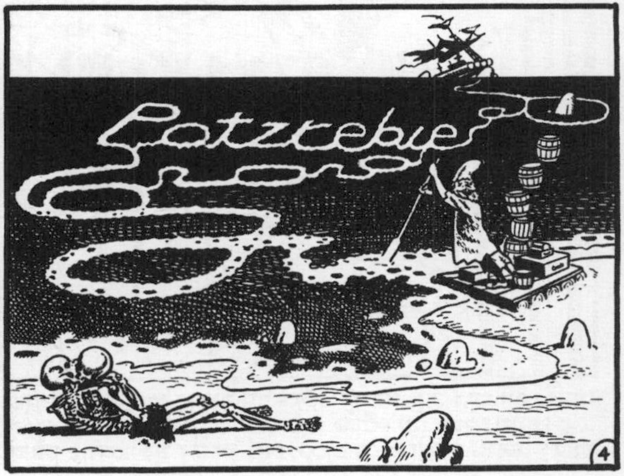
...without a moments hesitation, I was plunging in and out of the surf...and soon came back from the ship with another load of tools and another load of rum!

Realizing I might be on this island for a long time, I set about to the task of building quarters!... But since I had no ruler, I needed a rule to rule a ruler!

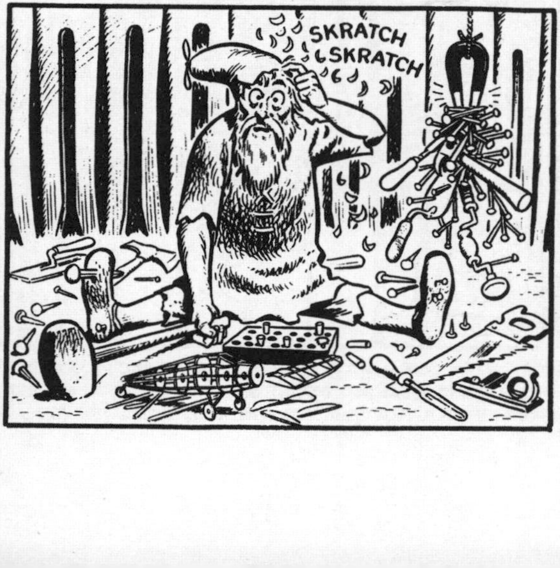
SKRATCH
SKRATCH

...and although I had the tools to make a ruler, I had no ruler to rule the straight edge for the ruler! So I cut a chunk of straight edge from the picture border!

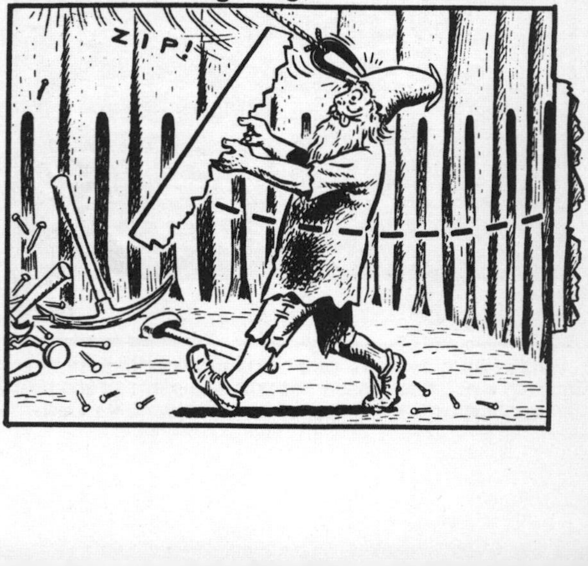
ZIP!

...which I might shape down to the final piece of work! I'm telling you...

...when I'd gotten it adzed down to a single board, I could then saw out a block...

...not having a whip-saw nor help, I'd chop my tree and shape it with an axe!

SCORE

Cutting wood for my projects was an unbeliev-able task! For example....

...it was ***more work*** making a ***mere toothpick*** than you could ever imagine!... But now, I had to give some thought to my living quarters!...I carefully chose my trees...

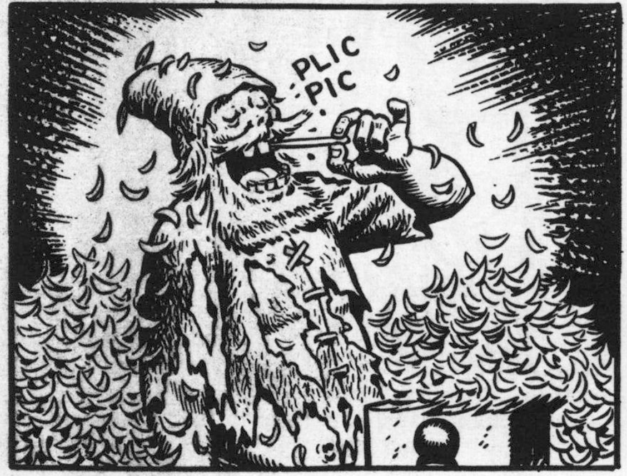
PLIC
PIC

...I then chopped a quantity of trees... trimmed shaped and adzed them on the spot to facilitate carrying them back to the site where I was building my quarters!

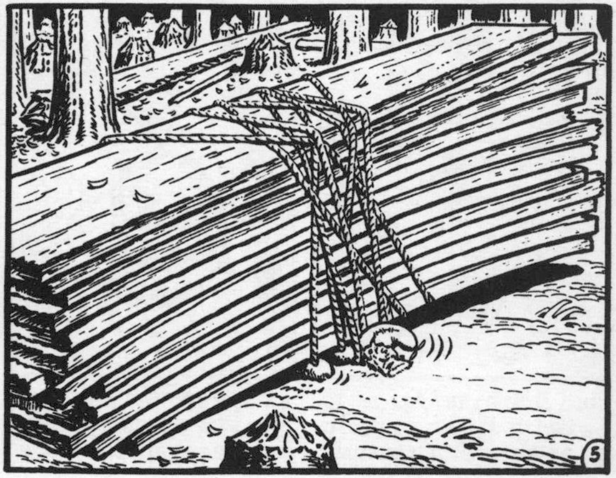
5

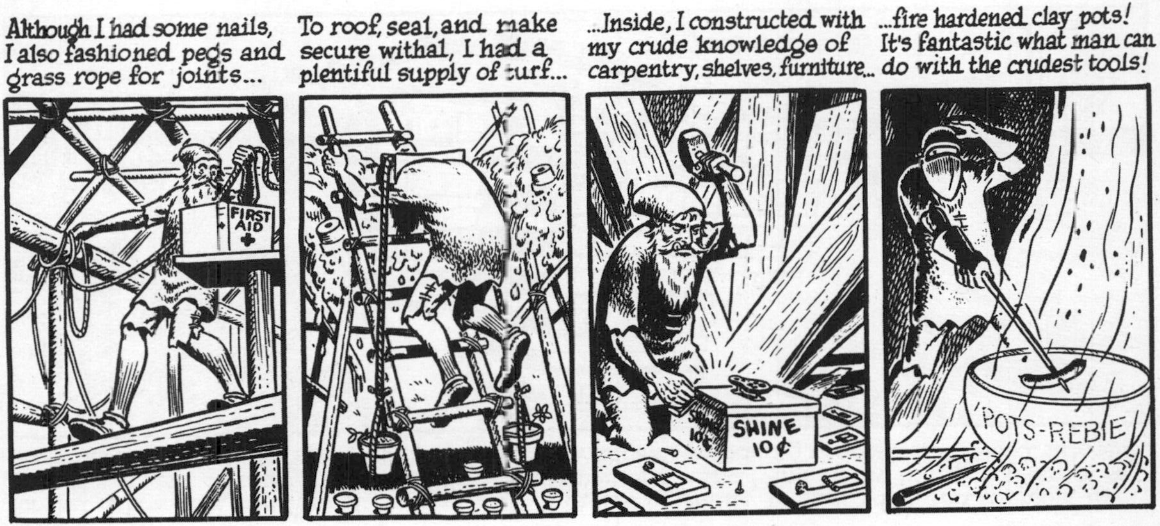
Although I had some nails, I also fashioned pegs and grass rope for joints...
FIRST AID
To roof, seal, and make secure withal, I had a plentiful supply of turf...
...Inside, I constructed with my crude knowledge of carpentry, shelves, furniture...
SHINE 10¢
...fire hardened clay pots! It's fantastic what man can do with the crudest tools!
POTS-REBIE

For that is how man is different from animal! Man has ingenuity to improvise and to make do with the crudest of tools... with the help of his hands and mind! And so, my living quarters rose above the island...a duplex apartment house...picture windows overlooking the sea... hollywood kitchens...

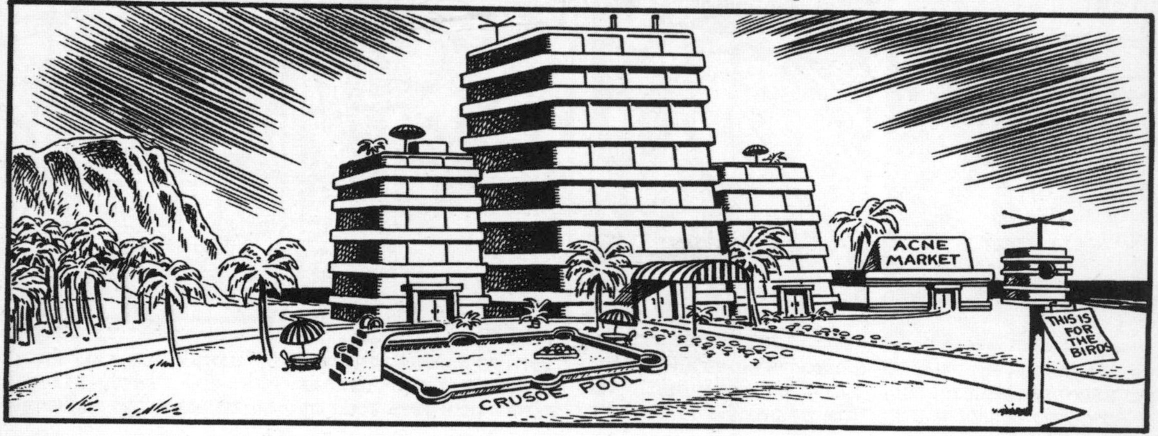
ACNE MARKET
THIS IS FOR THE BIRDS
CRUSOE POOL

Even though I was marooned alone on an island with only my wits to keep me going, I strangely enough began to feel quite at home, there in my duplex apartment...

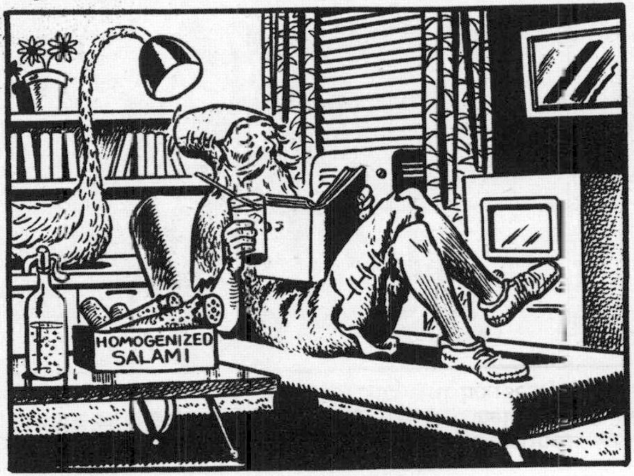
HOMOGENIZED SALAMI

...However, I was still *restless!* I needed to *build* one more thing...I needed one more item to make my living *complete!* I went for a ride in my hand built car!

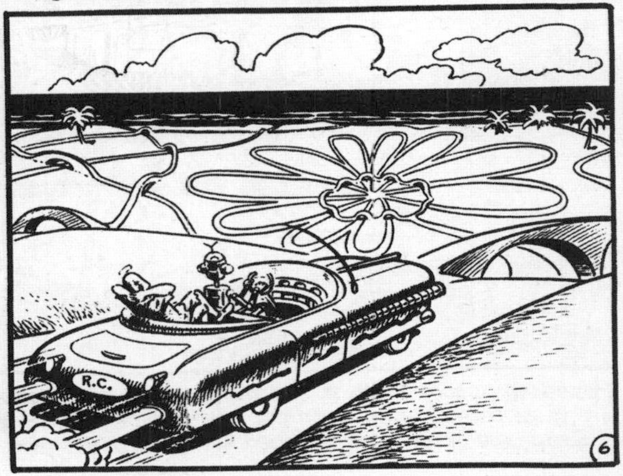
R.C.
6

After driving a while on my hand-built highway, I got out to walk on the shore! It was there that I came across what appeared to be a footprint.

Needless to say, I was perplexed at finding a solitary footprint in the sand! But upon closer examination, I observed it was no *footprint*...It was a *foot* in the sand!

A foot belonging to a native, who had been buried in the sand! He placed my foot on his head in gratitude...

...a gesture he regretted since I hadn't changed my sox in some time. He said his name was Friday... Joe Friday!

Said he was from Dragnet or something! However... this human being was the item I needed to make living complete!

Whats that you say? I needed Friday because I wanted someone to talk to?...Because I needed companionship? No! I merely wanted Friday's *brain*...

...hacked the beggar open ten seconds after I saved him! You see...I needed his brain to build the one more thing I needed to make my living complete...*WOMAN!*

I call her Francinestein...made of bits of grass rope...turf...goatskin...It's truly wonderful what man can do with the crudest of tools...

IN CASE OF FIRE BREAK GLASS.

THE LATE, LATE, LATE, LATE, LATE, LATE, LATE, LAIT, LEIGHT, LATE SHOW.

CRUNCH CRACK CRUNCH

MARK VII PRODUCTION

Report from Abroad—II: Continuing along the same sober lines that we did a few pages back, we devote this page, once more, to current events. You all can see by now, no doubt, that lying ahead of us is this future, and we must go forward to get there. And so, on this page, we go west to the Far East where things are really shaping up; our oriental correspondent has this to say . . .

脅威略侵俄蘇付

by 常備中西餅食咖

有無限的友好之感，我更常常讚佩
華民族的悠久文化與民族智慧，我
常讀美國賽珍珠女士關於描寫中國
著作，我認爲賽珍珠女士是美 Potrzebie
大的作家之一。
　親愛的執事先生，我希望用你這
筆告訴住在紐約的中國婦女們希望
們能抽出一部份寶貴的時間，寫信
這一位寂寞的中國婦人。她的中文
字叫「徐明君」，是一位極溫柔的
妻良母型的女子，她的通訊處是：

果能讀到她自己所認識的文字的話。
她一定會感到興奮的！此祝撰安！加
詩夫人寄自西德布萊梅城」。
Potrzebie（編者按）編者讀了加詩夫人這封
令人感動的信以後。除了感謝她的熱
誠以及對中國友好的誠意以外，我們
還從郵局寄了一些書報雜誌給留居德
國小鄉鎮中的徐明君女士，歐洲因爲
華僑人數極少，尚沒有鉛印的華文報
紙。我們決定以後經常寄一点報紙過
去，同時盼僑界人士能夠寫信給她！

在上海與一位名字叫作保羅披
德國商人結婚，雖然披爾士先
齡比她大得很多。但結婚以後
的愛情彌篤。她生了三個小孩
因爲善於經商，在上海渦著相
的生活，但戰 Potrzebie，共產
了上海。他們喪失了一切財產
被驅逐離開中國大陸，返回德
過轉輾的流浪，他們帶著叁個
西德一座叫作各民族之混合編
裏定居了下來，但是衛大不佑

中國婦人伴著叁個孩十，依靠於政府
的非薄救濟金過活，不特此也，她不
懂講德語，也聽不懂旁人講德語，她
只能講中國的上海本地話，生活環境
和風土人情完全與東方隔膜。無比的
寂寞籠罩著她那個殘破的家庭，她遂
漸消瘦憔弱而喪失生命的活力。我（
婦自稱）讀了那段德國報紙的新聞
以後，一夜不能入睡，我爲那位可憐
的數千英里外的遠東婦人的遭遇
，而感到衷心難過。她除了物質生活

報編輯部，昨晨接獲一不相識
老婦從西德布米梅海港寄來以
寫的信函 Potrzebie 婦署名加詩
內容述及一華婦在德種種，譯
：「紐約民氣日報館執事先生：
爲了一位值得同情的中國婦人
，我冒昧寫這封信給你，事情
是這樣的：幾天以前，我在西
報紙上，讀到關於一段那位中
的記述，她現在住在西德一個
小的事實是，很多年以前

SCIENCE DEPT: YOU EVER WATCH ONE OF THESE SPORTS NEWSREELS WHERE THEY'VE SPED UP THE CAMERA TO SLOW DOWN THE ACTION? .·. BY GEORGE, THERE'S MORE GOES ON IN AN ACTION THAN MEETS THE EYE! . . . LIKE FORINSTANCE, LET US SHOW YOU WHAT HAPPENS TO A GOLF BALL, BY GEORGE (THAT'S GEORGE DOWN THERE) . . . WHEN THE GOLF CLUB STRIKES IT IN

SLOW MOTION!

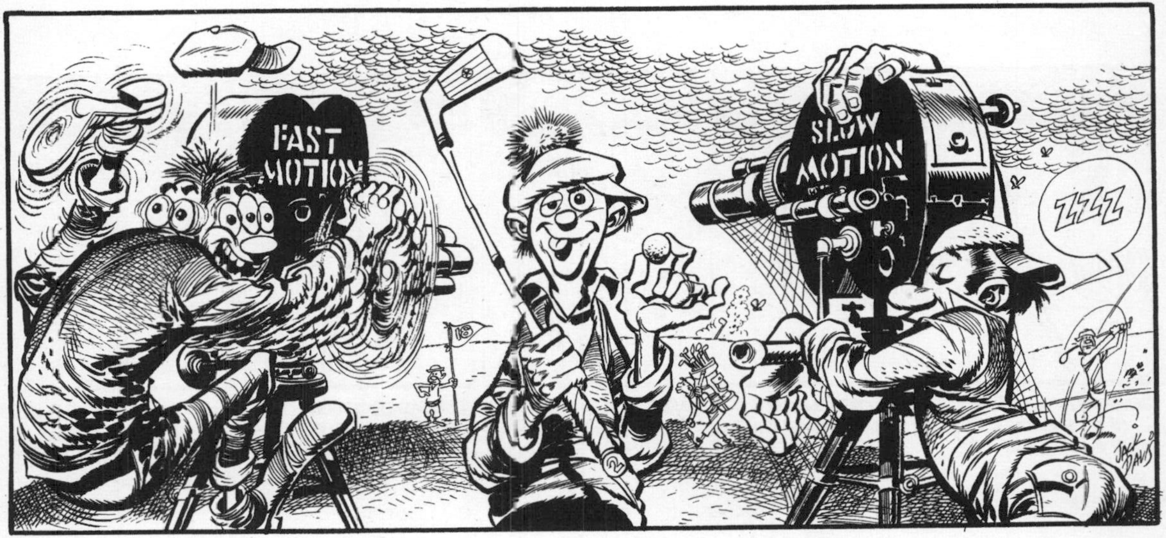
FAST MOTION
SLOW MOTION
ZZZ
JACK DAVIS

GOLF: HERE IS AN ORDINARY GOLF BALL ON A TEE!
...FROM THE RIGHT, THE GOLF CLUB APPROACHES ON DOWNWARD SWING!
...HERE, THE POINT OF CONTACT, WHERE CLUB TOUCHES SURFACE OF BALL...
...NOTE INTERESTING PHENOMENON CAUGHT BY THE SLOW-MOTION CAMERA...
...NOTE HOW SIDE OF GOLF BALL FLATTENS AN IN-STANT BEFORE LEAVING TEE!

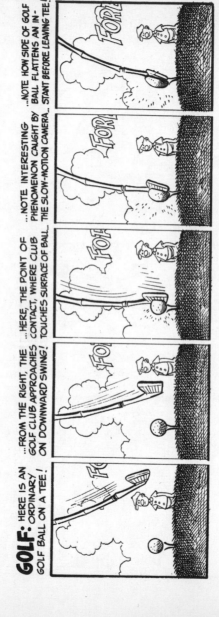

...STILL FLATTENING, BENDING THE CLUB AN INSTANT BEFORE LEAVING THE TEE...
FORE
...FLATTENING, BENDING... ANY MINUTE BALL IS ABOUT TO LEAVE TEE...
FORE
...BENDING, FLATTENING BENDING... ABOUT TO ANY MINUTE LEAVE...
FORE
...BENDING, LEAVING BENDING...
...**HEY WHAT THE HECK...**
RE
...SOMEONE NAILED THE BALL INTO THE GROUND, BY GEORGE!

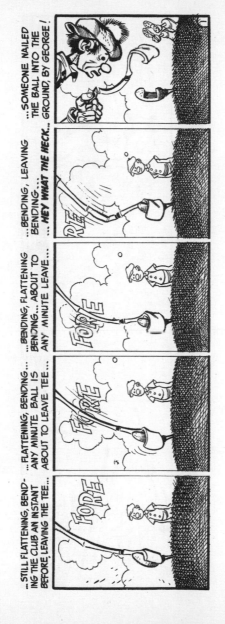

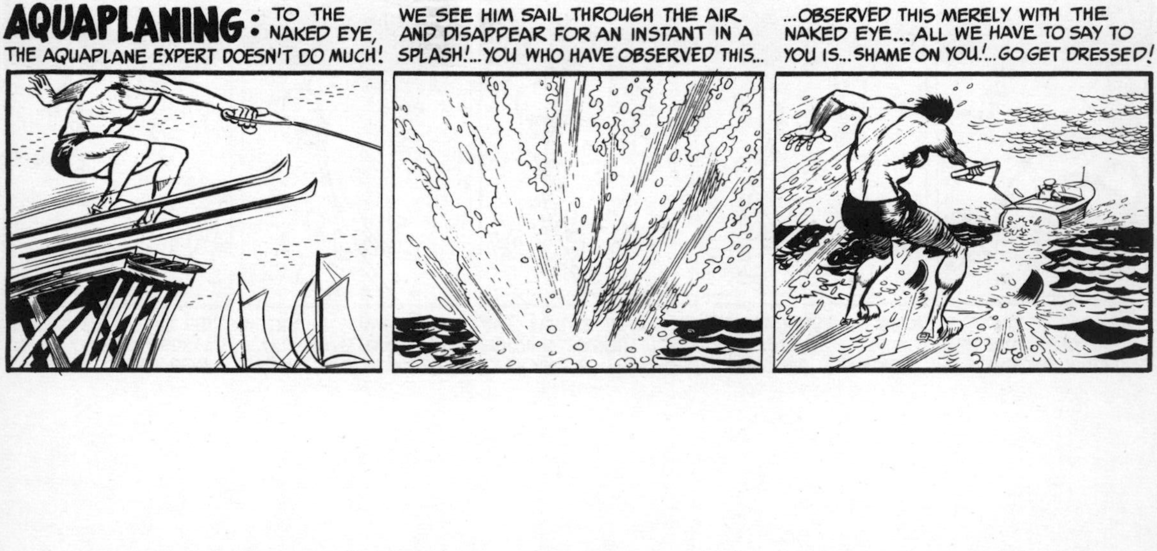
AQUAPLANING: TO THE NAKED EYE, THE AQUAPLANE EXPERT DOESN'T DO MUCH!
WE SEE HIM SAIL THROUGH THE AIR AND DISAPPEAR FOR AN INSTANT IN A SPLASH!...YOU WHO HAVE OBSERVED THIS...
...OBSERVED THIS MERELY WITH THE NAKED EYE... ALL WE HAVE TO SAY TO YOU IS...SHAME ON YOU!...GO GET DRESSED!

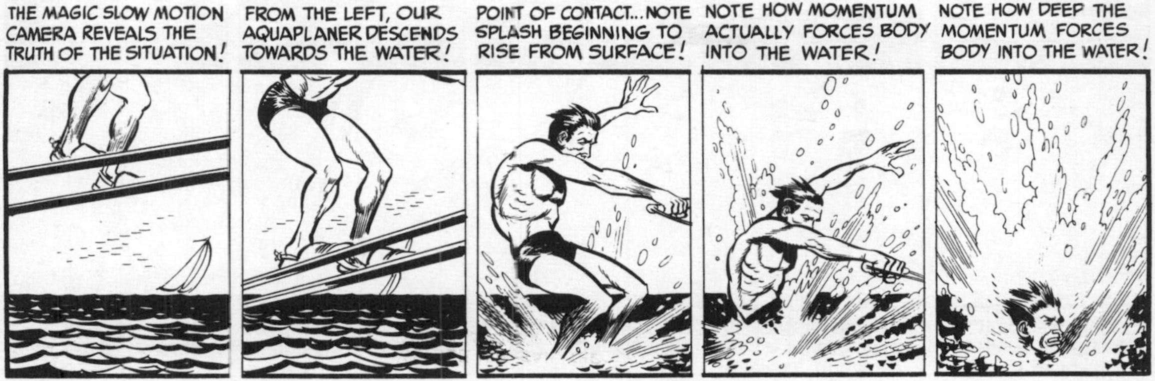
THE MAGIC SLOW MOTION CAMERA REVEALS THE TRUTH OF THE SITUATION!
FROM THE LEFT, OUR AQUAPLANER DESCENDS TOWARDS THE WATER!
POINT OF CONTACT...NOTE SPLASH BEGINNING TO RISE FROM SURFACE!
NOTE HOW MOMENTUM ACTUALLY FORCES BODY INTO THE WATER!
NOTE HOW DEEP THE MOMENTUM FORCES BODY INTO THE WATER!

NOTE IN FACT HOW THE BODY GOES COMPLETE-LY UNDER WATER ...
NATURALLY... ALL THIS HAPPENS SO FAST THE NORMAL EYE MISSES IT!
...I MEAN, IT MAY LOOK SLOW IN SLOW MOTION... ACTUALLY IT'S FAST!
...ACTUALLY, THE BODY TAKES A FRACTION OF A SECOND TO BOB UP!
...THIS IS ACTUALLY ALL HAPPENING IN A FRACTION OF A SECOND...

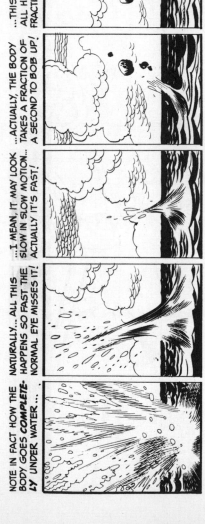

DON'T FORGET... THIS IS ACTUALLY A SLOW MOTION PICTURE...
...AND ANY SECOND, THE BODY WILL COME TO THE SURFACE ACTUALLY...
... ANY SECOND, TO THE SURFACE WILL ACTUALLY THE BODY COME...
...WELL HOW DO YOU LIKE THAT?... TSK TSK TSK!
BY GEORGE... THE BOAT BY MISTAKE WENT INTO THE SHALLOWS!
3

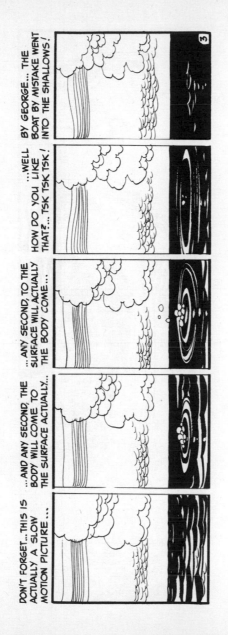

SWIMMING: NOW IN SWIMMING, WHEN THESE CHAMPIONS JUMP OFF THE DIVING BOARD, WHAT NORMAL HUMAN EYE CAN CATCH ALL THE GYRATIONS THEY DO IN ONE DIVE?

THE MAGIC YOU-KNOW-WHAT COMES TO OUR ⊘*м@# RESCUE!

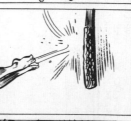

...HERE THE DIVER LEAVES THE BOARD IN A PER-FECT "SWAN DIVE"/!

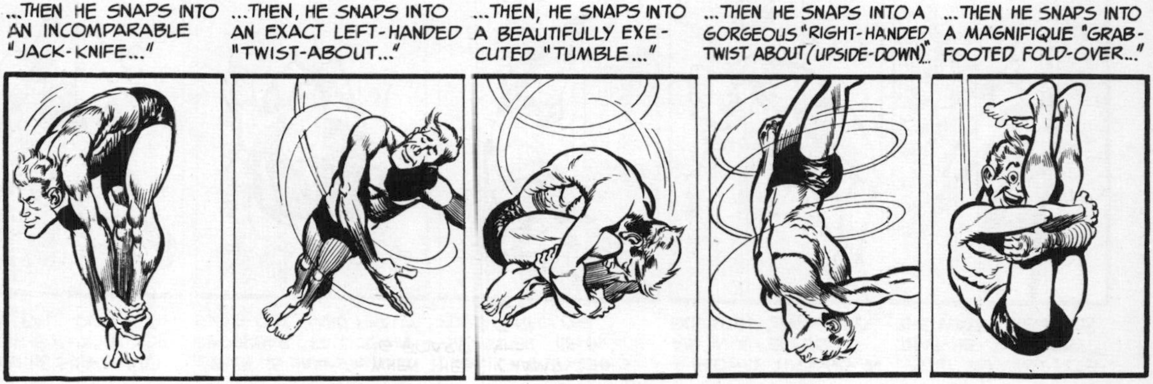
...THEN HE SNAPS INTO AN INCOMPARABLE "JACK-KNIFE..."
...THEN, HE SNAPS INTO AN EXACT LEFT-HANDED "TWIST-ABOUT..."
...THEN, HE SNAPS INTO A BEAUTIFULLY EXE-CUTED "TUMBLE..."
...THEN HE SNAPS INTO A GORGEOUS "RIGHT-HANDED TWIST ABOUT (UPSIDE-DOWN)"...
...THEN HE SNAPS INTO A MAGNIFIQUE "GRAB-FOOTED FOLD-OVER..."

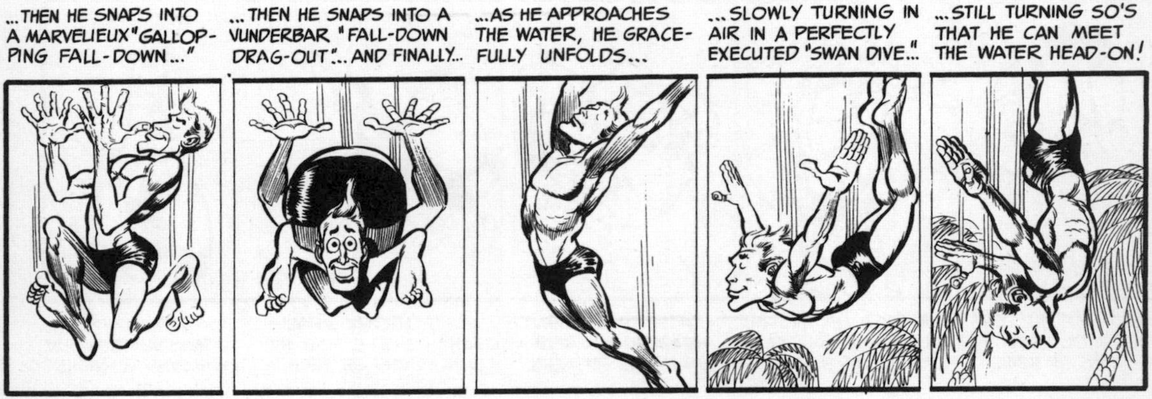
...THEN HE SNAPS INTO A MARVELIEUX "GALLOP-PING FALL-DOWN..."
...THEN HE SNAPS INTO A VUNDERBAR "FALL-DOWN DRAG-OUT"... AND FINALLY...
...AS HE APPROACHES THE WATER, HE GRACE-FULLY UNFOLDS...
...SLOWLY TURNING IN AIR IN A PERFECTLY EXECUTED "SWAN DIVE..."
...STILL TURNING SO'S THAT HE CAN MEET THE WATER HEAD-ON!

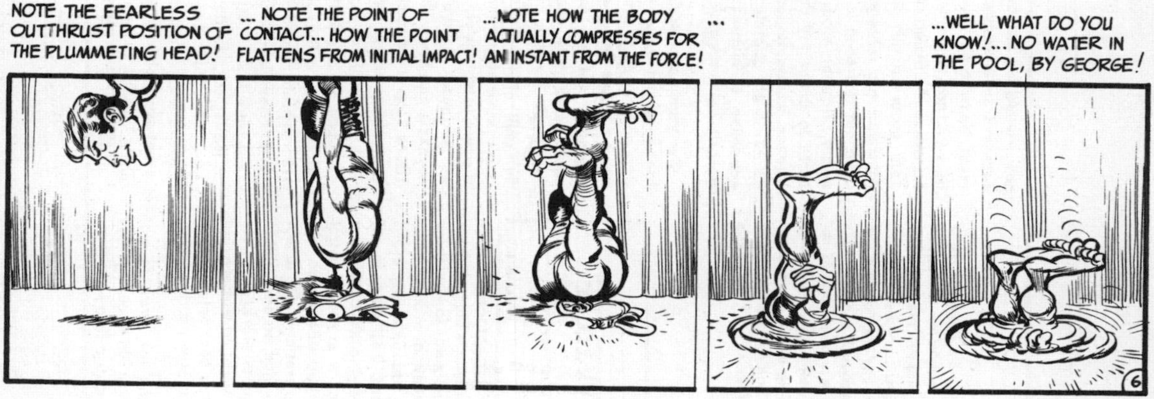
NOTE THE FEARLESS OUTTHRUST POSITION OF THE PLUMMETING HEAD!
... NOTE THE POINT OF CONTACT... HOW THE POINT FLATTENS FROM INITIAL IMPACT!
...NOTE HOW THE BODY ACTUALLY COMPRESSES FOR AN INSTANT FROM THE FORCE!
...
...WELL WHAT DO YOU KNOW!... NO WATER IN THE POOL, BY GEORGE!
6

Report from Abroad—III: This is the last of a series of serious articles on the serious subject of current events. We all know about large nations . . . we've heard from the Near East and the Far East. But what about the backward nations of the world. We always hear of backward nations, but never hear from backward nations. The following article, then, is the commentary of a leading analyst from a leading backward nation . . . an article entitled . . .

DRAWROF

by Yeldrums Serutan

Acitratna, sa ew llac eht tnenitnoc ni eht noiger fo eht Htuos Elop, seil yleritne rednu eci. Eht etis fo eht Htuos Elop si morf a dnasuoht ot owt- dnasuoht teef peed htaeneb siht digirf liam. dnA fo eht 000,41 selim fo eht latnenitnoc tsaoc ylno 000,4 selim era eerf morf eci, hcihw ni escalp smrof suomrone nekorbnu stfilc gnicaf eht aes, sderdnuh fo teef hgih. Dima siht enecs fo lanrete dloc, sa ew kniht fo ti, taerg sniatnuom worht pu rieht sdaeh. Emos fo meht sa Subere dna Rorret, era evitca seonaclov, gnivil secnruf derevoc htiw eci dna wons.

Eht egdelwonk ew evah fo siht trap fo eht htrae si eht tluser fo erom neht a yrutnec dna a flah fo etarep-sed rovaedne. Eht tneicna Skeerg demaerd fo a etarepmet tnenitnoc ereht. Neve ta eht dne fo eht htneethgie yrutnec, nem llits deveileb ni sti ecnatsixe. Acitratna si a tnenitnoc, a dnal ssam sa gib sa Eporue dna Ailartsua tup rehtegot. Dna ti saw ecno eht riaf dnal fo eht s'regayov noisiv. Hguoht erom neht shtrouf-eerht fo ti era tey drotnu yb nam, lareves smaes fo loac evah neeb dnuof no eht dnalniam, gnivorp eht ecnatsixe fo suoiruxul stserof dna gnizalb enihsnus ni sega gnol oga.

Ew yam emos yad wrad laoc rof taeh morf siht dnal fo eht ulfraef tsorf dna gnizylarap drazzilb. Ni tcaf, eht nosaer hcihw degru eht laicremmoc sreenoip otni eht saes taht hsaw eseht serohs saw eht deen rof taeh dna thgil. Ew dah on sag neht; lio saw eht ecruos fo thgil, dna slaes dna selahw erew eht ecruos fo lio. Os ti saw Drawhtuos oh! taht nem tnew, no lufdaerf segayov fo pihsdrah, ssenkcis dna lirep. Eht hcraes rof eht Htuos Elop si ton decart otni eht dim tnatsid seirutnec. Deedni, nehw ni 7481 Wemolohtrob Zaid delias dnuor eht Epac Nroh, yldrah enoyna ni eht dlrow evag a thguoht ot eht sdnal rehtraf htuos. Erofeb taht, srehpargoeg dah deveileb taht Areit Led Ogeuf (eht Dnal fo Erif) htuos fo eht Tiarts fo Nallegam saw detcennoc yltcerid htiw eht Wen Aeniug tsaoc. Tub Sekard egayov edam nem kniht taht ereht tsum eb a taerg dnalhtuos ro Driht Dlrow erehwemos ni eht nownk-un snoiger fo eht Htuos Elop.

Also available from ibooks:

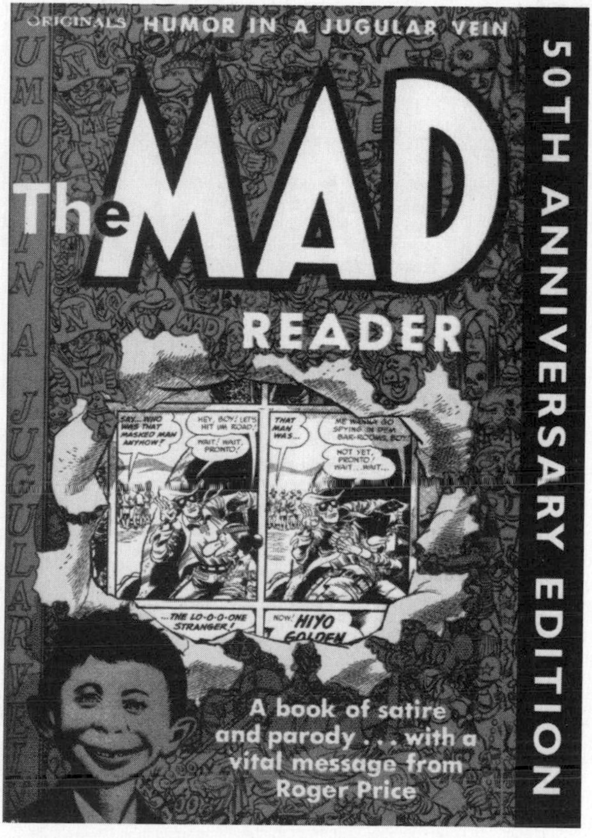

HUMOR IN A JUGULAR VEIN
The MAD
READER
50TH ANNIVERSARY EDITION
HEY, BOY! LET'S HIT UM ROAD!
THAT MAN WAS...
NOT YET, PRONTO! WAIT... WAIT...
...THE LO-O-O-ONE STRANGER!
NOW! HIYO GOLDEN
A book of satire and parody . . . with a vital message from Roger Price

The MAD Reader

ORIGINALS
More Humor in a Jugular Vein
MAD
STRIKES BACK!
With a Straight Talk by
50TH ANNIVERSARY EDITION

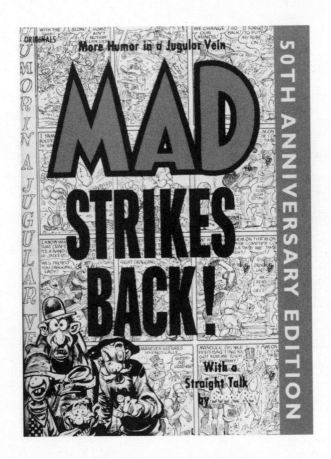

MAD Strikes Back!

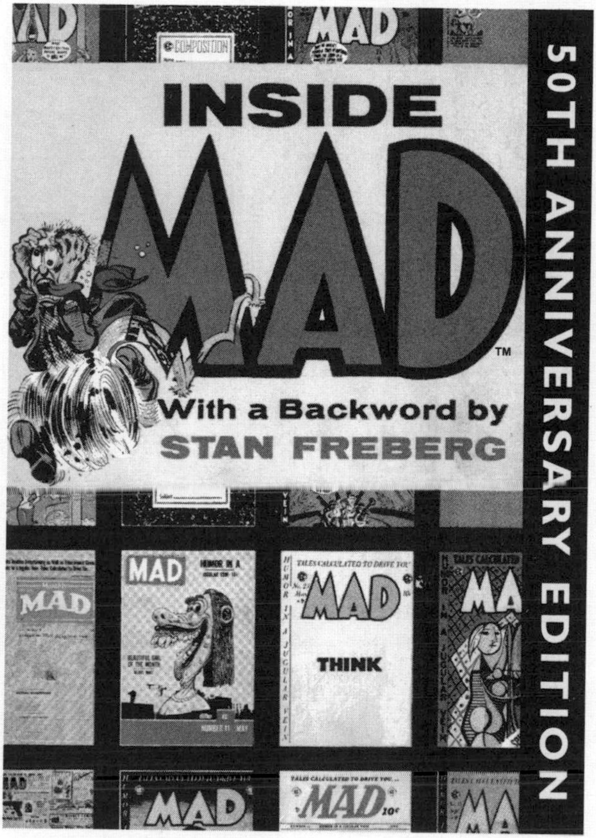
INSIDE
MAD
With a Backword by
STAN FREBERG
50TH ANNIVERSARY EDITION
THINK

Inside MAD

BEER
William M. Gaines'
UTTERLY
MAD
TM
50TH ANNIVERSARY EDITION
4th Superb Collection!

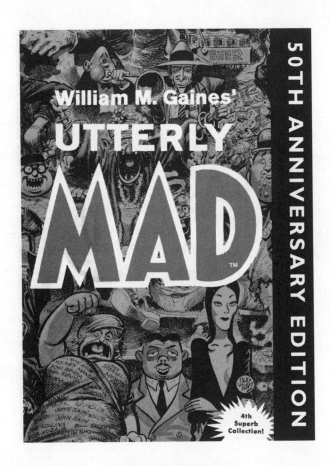

Utterly MAD

William M. Gaines'
THE BROTHERS
MAD
TM
50TH ANNIVERSARY EDITION
5 th Superb Collection!

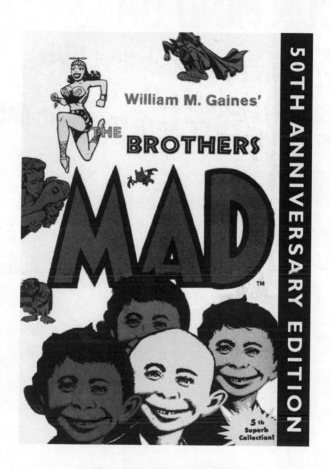

The Brothers MAD

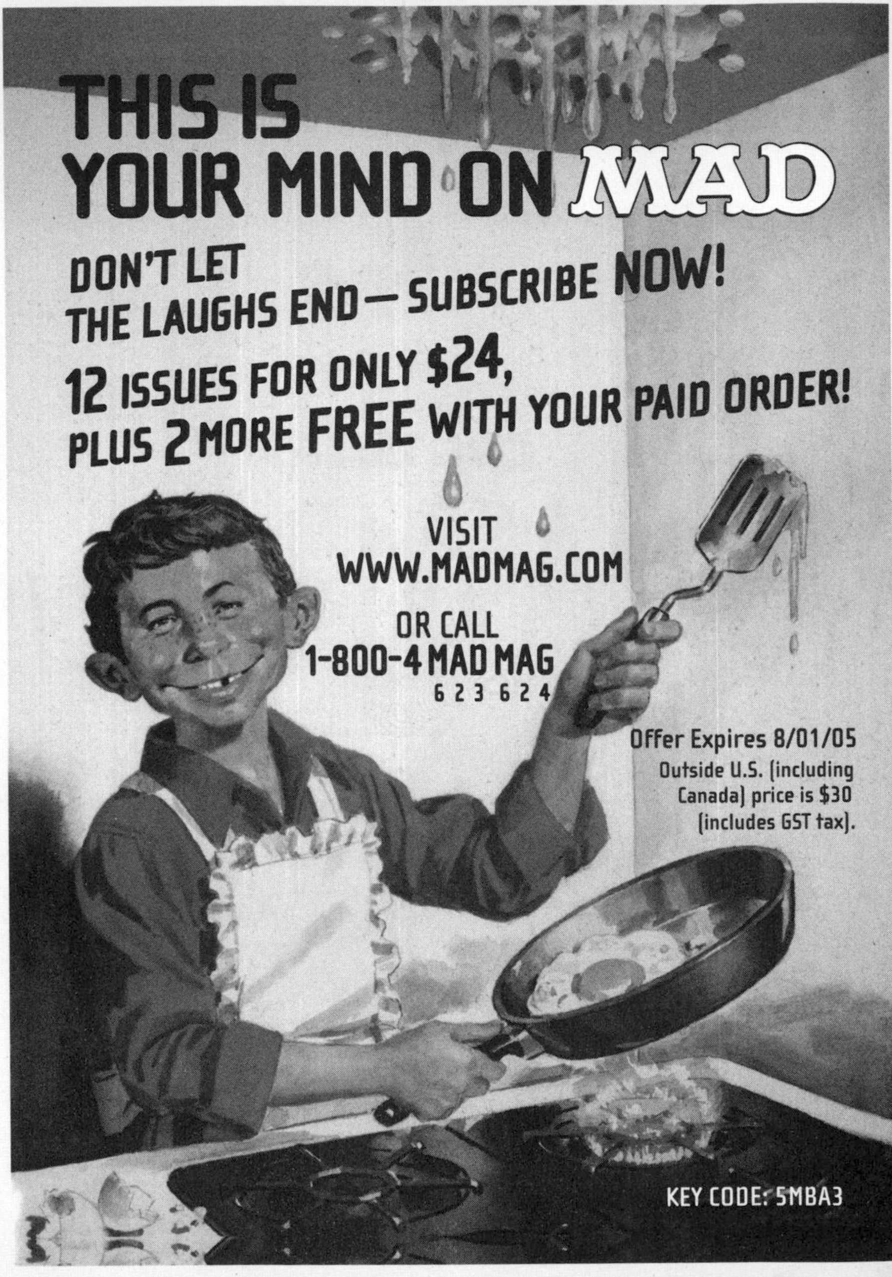

THIS IS
YOUR MIND ON MAD
DON'T LET
THE LAUGHS END— SUBSCRIBE NOW!
12 ISSUES FOR ONLY $24,
PLUS 2 MORE FREE WITH YOUR PAID ORDER!
VISIT
WWW.MADMAG.COM
OR CALL
1-800-4 MAD MAG
6 2 3 6 2 4
Offer Expires 8/01/05
Outside U.S. (including
Canada) price is $30
(includes GST tax).
KEY CODE: 5MBA3